NASHUA

People and Places

An anonymous quote reflects this book:

"If we could put our memories in a book of people and places we once knew, and take them out to remember the faces and the things we like to do, the glimpses of the past would brighten all our days and cause us to recall how wonderful the years have been and the meaning of it all."

A group gathered in front of the Hunt Memorial Building, Library Hill

Over the years, downtown Nashua has been a gathering place for people celebrating numerous events. The image on the cover shows Main Street, looking north, with the Hunt Memorial Building and the First Church in the background. The photograph is from the collection of The Nashua Historical Society.

NASHUA

PEOPLE AND PLACES

Meri Goyette
and
**The Nashua
Historical Society**

Published by Jetty House
an imprint of
Peter E. Randall Publisher
Portsmouth, NH

Copyright © 2011 Meri Goyette and the Nashua Historical Society
All rights reserved.

Published by Jetty House
An imprint of Peter E. Randall Publisher
Box 4726, Portsmouth, NH 03802-4726
www.perpublisher.com

(ISBN 13) 978-0-9828236-9-9
(ISBN 10) 0-9828236-9-X

Library of Congress Control Number: 2011936197

Composition by Ed Stevens Design
www.edstevensdesign.com

Contents

Acknowledgments vii

Introduction viii

History of Nashua ix

1. The Entrepreneurs 1

2. The Assistors 29

3. The Communicators 57

4. The Providers 79

5. The Challengers 103

Bibliography 130

Index 131

A city comes to life because of its people. People (who through their personal endeavors and life work encompass honesty, compassion, ability, integrity, spirit, action, and vision) are the fabric of the city. Like the comforting city tree lights which brighten the dark, these mentioned individuals (and innumerable others) have benefited us all. *Nashua People and Places* is a celebration of all their lives.

Meri Goyette (sitting on back of bench) and friends: Bliss Woodruff, Betty Gimber, Sherry Dutzy, Joe and Shirley Sakey, Carolyn Gaudet

Authors' Note: *Since the book's inception in 2008, some information has changed. With the 2011 publication date, the authors have chosen to let the book reflect the passage of time.*

Acknowledgments

This book is the result of a collaborative effort among The Nashua Historical Society, the author and the many contributors who shared their personal experiences and photographs. Meri Goyette was instrumental in conceiving the idea of *Nashua People and Places*. Dr. Charles Goyette, her supportive husband, and Meri Reid, her daughter and angel, are recognized for their help, patience, and understanding.

Timothy Glenday gave assistance and insight. Cynthia Kyriax Burney provided dedication and commitment to the project. From The Nashua Historical Society, Beth McCarthy (curator), Barbara Bankeroff and Jackie Walker (museum collection technicians), and Frank Mooney (Nashua historian and collector of vintage material) added valuable expertise. Some photographs are from the Frank M. Ingalls collection and the Millennium Archival Photography Project of the Nashua Historical Society.

Thank you also to Patty Ledoux for sharing her love for Nashua, its history, and its people; Roland Lesieur, local businessman and owner of many collectable photographs and postcards; Robin Ann Peters for her technical skill; Dean Shalhoup, columnist of *The Telegraph*; Ralph Wright, photographer; Albert Wilkinson, photographer; Claire Young, photographer; Carol Eyman, Nashua Public Library Community Services coordinator, for recommending the publishing house of Peter E. Randall; Deidre Randall for providing personal consultation for the design and production of this publication; and the community at large whose lives are the city.

This book exists because of the generosity of Charles Goyette who made the publication of *Nashua People and Places* a reality.

INTRODUCTION

Nashua has often been called a "unique" city. Perhaps its dual honors—in 1987 and again in 1997—of being chosen the best place in America in which to live and to work by *Money* magazine, or its advantageous geographical placement which led to its steady growth since its incorporation as Dunstable Township more than 200 years ago, can be credited for this flattering description.

As any resident of even modest tenure can attest, at the root of Nashua's success, its ability to thrive in good times and ride out the lean years relatively unscathed, is most certainly its people.

Indeed, from the earliest homesteaders whose tireless toil transformed endless forests and sandy plains into productive fields of sustenance to the successful, community-minded citizenry that fed Nashua's momentum of positive growth and desirability into the 19th, 20th, and now the early 21st century, people have always been, and will always be, Nashua's greatest assets.

This compilation celebrates a select few of the many individuals whose contributions, from the private and subtle to the most public and heralded, gently guided Nashua close to the pinnacle of true community- the phrase that defines "success" for the tiniest Maine village and the bustling island of Manhattan alike.

In his book, *Better Together* NH Charitable Foundation president Lew Feldstein makes frequent reference to the term "social capital," which refers to the collective value of all social networks—those in "the know"—and the inclinations that arise from the networks to do things for each other. In short Feldstein, as a result of years of research and study on the subject, comes to the conclusion that communities can, and do, enjoy a wide variety of very specific benefits when its people employ trust, reciprocity, information, and cooperation in their daily lives.

Certainly, Nashua can be described as a community rich in social capital. The author is confident that by perusing this collection of names and faces, the reader will understand how Nashua grew into the quintessential New England city—no, community—that it is today.

—Dean Shalhoup

Nashua, New Hampshire…

The village that grew from a sparse settlement into a central point of business, art, and culture.

In the beginning, the township was called Dunstable. In 1837, its name became Nashua in recognition of the Nashua River, the waterway that was the engine that fueled the commercial and industrial growth of Nashua and its environs.

The village becomes a city, a major industrial center

Electric trolleys and a railroad system replaced horse cars, sleds, stagecoaches, and boats as forms of travel.

Cotton and woolen mills and a wide diversity of manufacturing companies brought an influx of Irish, French-Canadian, and Jewish immigrants and people from Poland, Greece, and Lithuania.

The Textile Mills leave Nashua

After over 120 years of continuous service, the mills closed in the late 1940s. The city was devastated.

Enter High Technology and Research

Sanders Associates was one of the first technology companies to come to Nashua, followed by other research, high technology, computer and software companies.

Growth and prosperity of the city continued with an influx of engineers, researchers, electronic technicians, administrators, and managers spurring the proliferation of professional and cultural institutions by explosive and unprecedented growth.

NASHUA PEOPLE AND PLACES

Remembering those who helped make Nashua what it is today.

—Joseph Sakey and Meri Goyette

ONE

THE ENTREPRENEURS

"Honesty, integrity and empathy are not personality characteristics that can be turned on and off at will. They are priceless and cannot be bought…They either exist or they don't."

Neil D. Koppenhaver
"Wind Devils"

City Hall

In 1853 Nashua was incorporated and the 1843 Town Meeting House became City Hall. There, local militia used the attic for meetings and drills; the Police Department was headquartered in the back. In 1926 a major leak showed great disrepair; the building was demolished along with the adjacent Municipal Records Building. A new City Hall was built with federal assistance. It was dedicated in November of 1938.

Dick Avard is a third generation Avard in the retail clothing industry. Originally the family business was established in 1924 at Besse Bryant Clothing Store on Main Street by Dick's grandfather, Nashua native Albert Avard. Avard then opened his own store run by son Raymond in the 1960s-70s. Dick took over operations in 1981 "carrying on with the same quality clothing."

Avard Store is to the left of the bank.

Banker Robert Cross joined the Nashua Trust Company in 1956 as assistant vice president. By 1973 he had become CEO and chairman of the board, remaining until the merger with Amoskeag Bank. He served as trustee of Memorial Hospital and as chairman of Rivier College trustees' board. He was president of the Humane Society, Greater Nashua Chamber of Commerce, and Rotary Club. In 1982 Cross was named Nashua's Citizen of the Year.

Nashua Trust Bank

The Entrepreneurs

After gaining cooking experience in Germany working with a master chef and running establishments in the Nashua area, chef Michael Buckley (with his wife and partner Sarah) opened Michael Timothy's Urban Bistro Wine and Jazz bar in 1995. Surf, serving upscale seafood, opened in 2002 and Merrimack's Buckley's Great Steaks opened in 2005. Specialties are always on the menu. Said Buckley, "We serve thoughtful, hearty, and creative dishes that aren't pretentious." Michael Timothy's is adjacent to the location of the old Colonial Theater. Across Main Street the Surf Restaurant is located in the 1930s Public Service Building, also the former location of the Coyote Café. This block had housed the Parkinson Building, site of historical news interest including the *Nashua Gazette* which had become a daily paper in 1872 and continued until 1895. Its successor was the *Nashua Daily Press*, published until 1905.

Michael Timothy's

Adam Mermer, great-grandson of Henri Burque, is carrying on the personal service and family tradition of jewelry. Opened in 1909, the store carries jewelry from around the world, pewter, porcelain and china giftware, fine writing instruments, watches, and clocks. Personalized service includes custom-design jewelry, as well as jewelry and watch repair. "No job is too small or too big" for Burque Jewelers.

Alec Koutsos (at age 21) and his father opened the original Alec's Shoe Store on West Pearl Street in 1938. Their belief was that "satisfied customers are the true measure of success in the retail trade." After a devastating fire in 1960, the store reopened on West Pearl Street. In 1995, Alec and his son John moved the business to Main Street. The three level, 40,000 square foot building allowed for brand expansion and an upstairs outlet. Alec's offers "shoes for the entire family" and continues to strive for customer satisfaction.

The Entrepreneurs

Most of the retail experience for the first seven decades of the 20th century was centered in downtown Nashua, especially the access to the corners of Main Street. Montgomery Ward, Marsh Parsons, and Sears & Roebuck all thrived along Main Street during this period. A prominent midpoint to this shopping experience was the intersection of Main Street with East and West Pearl streets. While the latest generations know the brick building as Alec's Shoe Store, for lifetime Nashuans this facility is best remembered as Miller's Department Store. Herb Miller was the longtime proprietor of this establishment, along with investments in other area businesses, including the old WOTW AM & FM radio station located on Lund Road. For his many contributions to the community, Herb Miller was named in the 1990s "Man of the Year" by the Greater Nashua Chamber of Commerce. Before its closing, Miller's was managed by Herb's son Ken.

YMCA, Prospect Street

John Carter of the architectural firm Carter and Woodruff was involved in many school designs and local buildings including YW/YMCA, Temple Beth Abraham, and the current Nashua Public Library. His father, Eliot Avery Carter, was director of the Second National Bank, a state representative and senator, and twice the Greater Nashua Chamber of Commerce Citizen of the Year. Among Eliot Carter's civic and philanthropic contributions was his donation for a new 57,000 square foot public library which opened in 1971 on Court Street. One of the benefactors and president of the trustees was Attorney Frank Clancy, for whom the proposed wing was to be named.

"Children Reading," a monument by Lloyd Lillie outside the Nashua Public Library, Court Street

THE ENTREPRENEURS

In 1947 father and son bakers Eugene and Jacob Crosby opened their bakery. Since 1957 Crosby Bakery has been on East Pearl Street. The family business, now run by daughter Gale and her husband Mike Cummings, still sells sweets as well as French-Canadian style meat pies and baked beans. Crosby Bakery has also added a breakfast and lunch menu with soups and sandwiches. "We still make everything from scratch," said Gale Cummings.

Crosby Bakery

1897 – 1898 Nashua Sport Team

Nashua has always enjoyed individual retail establishments. The Jauron family operated Jauron Sporting Goods for several decades near the corner of Amherst and Broad streets. Dick Jauron has not only provided footballs for the youth of Nashua from his uncle's store but also initiated football ideas as a National Football League coach, head coach, and coordinator in Detroit, Chicago, and Buffalo.

Retailer Jordan Cohen and his father opened Jordan's Luggage Shop in 1947. In 1958 a new building which presently houses Jordan's Luggage Shop opened. The store sells luggage, handbags, briefcases, wallets, trunks, other leather goods, umbrellas, and gift items like Hummels. Jordan's offers luggage repair and free 24-karat gold monogramming on store-purchased goods. "We've been doing business in downtown Nashua for sixty years and it has been a pleasure," Cohen said.

JORDAN'S LUGGAGE SHOP

89-95 MAIN STREET   NASHUA, N.H. 03060-2768   (603) 883-3911

Largest Luggage Specialty Shop in N. H.

Florist Charlie Fortin opened a floral shop in 1931, continuing today as Fortin-Gage Ltd. selling gifts and flowers. In 1965 Eddie Gage bought the business and sold it in 2000 to Jody, his son, and Jill Gage. Since 1968 Fortin-Gage has also become known for decorating the White House in Washington, D.C. Jody said Eddie taught him "the lesson of supporting the community, making a difference."

The White House, Washington, D.C.

THE ENTREPRENEURS

Peter Collins is the third generation of the family to own and operate Collins Flowers Inc, located on Main Street at the top of Library Hill. Established in 1930 the store not only sells floral arrangements but also stuffed animals, balloons, plants, dish gardens, and handcrafted fruit and gourmet baskets. "Joy and jealousy, desire and dejection, solitude and sadness, loyalty and love…flowers echo each voice of the human heart."

Decorated fireplace at the Hunt Memorial Library

Owners J and Judi (Ouellette) Goyette are the J and J of J&J Construction. Childhood sweethearts and Nashua High graduates, they achieved prominence in their field of endeavor by offering the home buyer creativity and elegance with contemporary styling in the development of their land and home construction.

The railroads have a significant role in the history of Nashua, and two major spurs crossed Main Street. One line, still active today, ran parallel to Canal Street along the river. The other, now converted to a rail trail for pedestrians, ran along East and West Hollis streets, and had several major loading docks. None was more prominent than the Nashua Beef Company, presided over by Larry Elliot and co-owned by Al Savage (known as "Mr. Elks"). Elliot also played a major role in the establishment of Bishop Guertin High School in 1963. The Nashua Beef Company eventually expanded, including the acquisition of a competitor in Concord, New Hampshire. Larry's large family produced headlines both for academics and success on the athletic field. For such devotion to greater Nashua as a family, a bust of Larry Elliot was commissioned, and along with a similar tribute to U.S. President John F. Kennedy, graces a downtown plaza so all will remember his generosity and warmth.

Entertainer and businessman Ken Darrell opened New Hampshire's first Darrell's Music Hall in 1970, introducing himself in a TV commercial wearing a red hat and calling himself Ken Santa Darrell (he had sung professionally). Soon he had stores in Nashua and Portsmouth selling pianos, sheet music, and organs. Through the years, he donated instruments to music schools, churches, and charities. Darrell was a family man teaching his children respect and community involvement. His son K.C. Darrell started in the business at eighteen moving pianos, next working at the Bedford Mall store trying to learn the business, and then running the store in West Lebanon, N.H. Now K.C. is company president of Darrell's Music Hall with three locations in Portsmouth, Concord, and Nashua (the flagship store). One rule still holds true: family always comes first.

Aerial view looking north, Main Street

As Nashua grew from 50,000 to 87,000 residents during the Eisenhower era, no business adapted to the times in quite the unique fashion of P E Fletchers. Selma and Bernie Pastor began selling modern appliances from an outlet in the middle of downtown. As the need to display more items and to expand the service department developed, they purchased the old A&P grocery store property at the corner of Main and Allds streets. With the changing of this area to professional buildings and restaurant space, their son David moved the facility, yet again, to the Amherst Street location. P E Fletchers currently occupies space some five miles west of downtown. The 21st century has seen the doubling of size at that location with easier access to automobiles.

The Entrepreneurs

James (Mitch) Fokas and his wife Ethel transformed a small lunch counter into a downtown Main Street landmark known as Martha's Sweet Shoppe, selling candy with specialties made for the holidays. Operated today by their sons Chris and Billy, it is known as Martha's Exchange. Their business is located in the Merchants Exchange Building which was completed in 1872 and is an example of Victorian buildings of the era housing paint and harness shops. The builder, coal merchant Jeremiah White, housed his drug store there. Other businesses included the 2nd National Bank headquarters (1875), Underhill Drug Company (early 1900s), and in the late 1920s the Tremont Theater, Ideal Lunch, and Trombloom's Men's Clothing. A 1930 fire damaged the building's north end. Upon completion of the restoration, the project was given the mayor's Blue Ribbon Award for excellence in the preservation of a historic building.

Charlie and Rita Forrence were married in 1941. After erecting a fence to protect their children from traffic, they were asked to build a neighbor's fence. From then everything went into their business, the Gate City Fence Company. Incorporated in 1947, the company moved in 1966 to Ledge Street which houses an on-site manufacturing facility. Today, sons Ken and Chicky, daughter Dru, and other family members work at the business.

Roland Lesieur's father, Leo Lesieur, opened the Maynard & Lesieur garage in 1928 with three gas pumps. Then the service station offered gasoline, light repairs, and car maintenance. Still in the same location the business is the area's 'tire specialist' with an inventory for cars, trucks, motorcycles, trailers, and ATV's. R. Lesieur has been elected to the New England Tire Dealers Hall of Fame. Today Maynard and Lesieur is a family business.

Of Samuel A. Tamposi, it has been said, "He was a man who grew up poor and had a great love of the land. He loved to build things, things that would be of value" (Senator Warren Rudman). He was "unafraid to take risks" (*Nashua Telegraph*). Tamposi, son of Romanian immigrants and a Nashua native, was raised on the family farm. From farmer and after several years as a vacuum cleaner salesman, he began buying vacant Nashua mill buildings, factories, and farmland. These purchases were the foundations of his real estate holdings from New Hampshire to Florida. Tamposi met Gerald Nash and the two formed a partnership, becoming New Hampshire's largest real estate developers. Many Fortune 500 companies subsequently built plants in the state. Tamposi's interest in baseball led to a limited partnership in the Boston Red Sox and a friendship with Ted Williams. Citrus Hills, a Florida community, was developed in the late 1960s. Tamposi, a Republican Party activist, was instrumental in many local, state, and national campaigns.

Engineer Royden C. Sanders, Jr., Mort Goulder, and nine other engineers in 1952 began a high-tech operation in an abandoned textile mill on Canal Street. Sanders himself also designed innumerable devices that promoted both business and military technology. In the business world, engineer Mort Goulder is known for investing in start-up companies. Goulder served his country most notable as Assistant U.S. Secretary of Defense and was named the 2007 Greater Nashua Chamber of Commerce Citizen of the Year.

Sanders Associates Inc., now a part of BAE Systems North America, outgrew its complex on Canal Street and moved its headquarters to Spit Brook Road as well as adding additional plants in Nashua, Merrimack, Hudson, and for several years in Manchester. The boom years at Sanders meant developing everything from top secret components for the military to the "Wizard of Avis" computerized car reservation system.

Royden C. Sanders, Jr.

Millyard, Nashua

Grandson of the founder of a practical system of making shipping and storage containers leading to the founding of International Paper Box Machine Company (located at the Vale Mill site), Philip LaBombarde worked in the family business, ultimately becoming its president. Serving as director of the Nashua Airport Authority and chairman of St. Joseph's Hospital, LaBombarde was a state Constitutional Convention delegate and a New Hampshire General Court representative. On the Vale Mills site, there were earlier mills such as the 1823 Nashua Manufacturing Company and the 1825 Indian Head Company specializing in cotton fabric production. Many laborers had left area farms to work in the mills but found the companies controlled every aspect of their lives. For many reasons by the late 1940s, the textile industry in the North had faltered and then failed.

Robert Lavoie and his son Steve are only the third family owners of C.H. Avery, a business selling furniture which has remained unchanged for more than 100 years. Spanning three centuries, Avery Furniture Store was opened in 1887 by Charles Holman Avery who started selling furniture to both merchants and mill hands. In 1925 Avery sold the business to three of his employees: Davis, Brooks, and David Pinet. The partly wood-framed store on Factory Street was rebuilt into a five-story masonry structure after a fire in 1925; two levels are below the street. Pinet's son Paul began working in the store in 1930. Paul sold the store to Lavoie in 1992. As a youth Lavoie had worked in his father's store, Eddie's Bedding and Furniture, which had opened in 1952. Upon purchase of Avery's he consolidated both stores in the Avery Building. The Lavoies' philosophy is to offer better service than department stores and chain furniture stores, to place special custom orders, and to satisfy customers.

The Entrepreneurs

Vacchi Manoukian, local developer, purchased St. Francis Xavier Church on Chandler Street with the intent of giving it to the Armenian community. The church, erected in 1886 by Alphonse Chagnon, is on an elevation commanding views of the city. The first marble church to be built in the state, it is of Norman style with a Latin cross floor plan.

Sy Mahfuz is owner of Persian Rug Galleries. In memory of his father Fouad who founded the business in 1953, Mahfuz donated an 11X18 foot ivory Kashan carpet to the lobby of the Hunt Building on Library Hill. Of his father Mahfuz said, "He believed the community is a big family in which we all share responsibilities and success alike." Mahfuz's son Fouad has joined the family business.

Sy Mahfuz

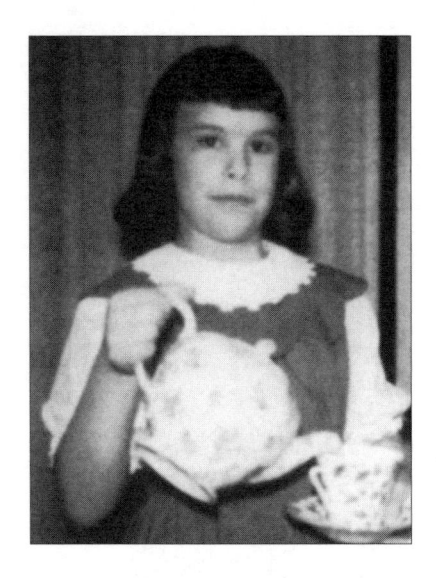

It was January 1979 that owners Don and Meri Reid began their legacy of customer service with "quality, consistency, and value" as the motto of the Common Crossing Restaurant in downtown Nashua. Meri set the bar for customer service while Don wrote menus that paved the way for culinary creativity in Nashua. The Reids continue their customer-first approach as a team at Prudential Verani Realty.

A young Meri Reid

Three generations of the LaRose family owned and operated the Modern Restaurant in downtown Nashua. The Modern was best known for that friendly feeling one gets from home-style cooking combined with homespun storytelling. Dick LaRose has revealed the Modern restaurant's secret. "We always had a special blend of coffee, a better quality from our wholesaler, than what the other area restaurants were willing to pay for."

The Entrepreneurs

Peter, left, and Philip Scontsas

Peter Scontsas, a long time Main Street merchant, began working in a shoe-repair shop which evolved into Scontsas and Sons Greeting Cards. In 1974 a jewelry store was added. Referring to himself as "Pete the Greek on Main Street," he was instrumental in joining the city's two Greek churches into St. Philip Greek Orthodox Church. The second annual stroll was dedicated to Scontsas, "Mr. Downtown." Philip Scontsas, Peter's son, has been involved in the family business since his teen years. He is a Graduate Gemologist. In 1995 Philip and his wife Amalia founded their home décor department to complement the long-running jewelry store, now known as Scontsas Fine Jewelry and Home Décor. Scontsas is active in many merchant initiatives including the Great American Downtown, Taste of Nashua, and downtown holiday tree lighting.

Philip and Amalia Scontsas

Following college, John Stabile II entered Nashua construction. His success has been recognized by *Business NH Magazine* on three occasions when compiling a list of the ten most powerful New Hampshire people. Founded as H.J. Stabile and Son, Inc. in 1973, the general contracting firm now known as the Stabile Company has integrated commercial and industrial work with civic endeavors. John has served the community on the Board of Aldermen and as a New Hampshire State Senator. He has accepted many appointments to industrial boards from both the city and the state. For example, he has served as a Nashua Police Commissioner. Civically, he is well known as a Boys Club Director, a Rivier College Trustee, and an owner of the minor league baseball franchise, the Nashua Pride. Stabile has more than once served as a campaign's financial chairman in the Granite State.

Electrical contractor James Stellos founded Stellos Electric in 1954 which is now headquartered on Industrial Boulevard. Stellos, a leader in St. Philip Greek Orthodox Church, served on the Hellenic College Board and received the Diocesan Award from the church's Boston Diocese. In the early 1980s he partnered with Gerald Nash, Nashua Construction LLC. From its Temple Street offices, Nash has specialized in industrial, office, retail, and medical renovations. The two men built a broadcast facility in Derry with a 510 foot communication tower in Hudson and operated New Hampshire's second commercial TV station, WNDS, for over thirty years. Many area charities and civic groups have looked to the foundations these two companies have established for support. A new youth-oriented, rectangular sports field located off Route 3 Exit 5 West was named after Stellos.

Old-time Nashuans remember the Yankee Flyer Diner. The 1997 James Aponovich mural, the result of a fund raising drive by Meri Goyette, depicts a 1940s–50s scene filled with local residents. Chris Kyriax was the owner. Upon his death in 1952, his wife Mary Anne operated the diner which closed in 1965. Others in the mural are listed in the accompanying plaque along with a brief description. The Yankee Flyer was one of three diners, located at the intersection of East-West Hollis and Main streets. The other two were Henry's and the Rosebud originally operated by the Bartas family. Beginning in the 1900s when 25 cents would buy you a dinner (or 20 cents for the weekly meal-ticket system) the diner was a local destination of many.

Yankee Flyer Diner Mural

Referred to as a "Main Street icon" by a local columnist, city barber Rino Long joined the original Chuck's Barber Shop in 1959. Buying the business in 1984, he moved the shop to another Main Street location. Long is remembered for his kindness to all, especially those in the military and law enforcement.

Frederick Shaw joined J.F. McElwain Shoe Company rising through the ranks to Vice President. He was involved in community affairs at many levels including the Industrial Management Club, the YMCA, and the Bicentennial Celebration. As Deacon of The First Church, Shaw donated a much needed chapel. He was married to Muriel Evans.

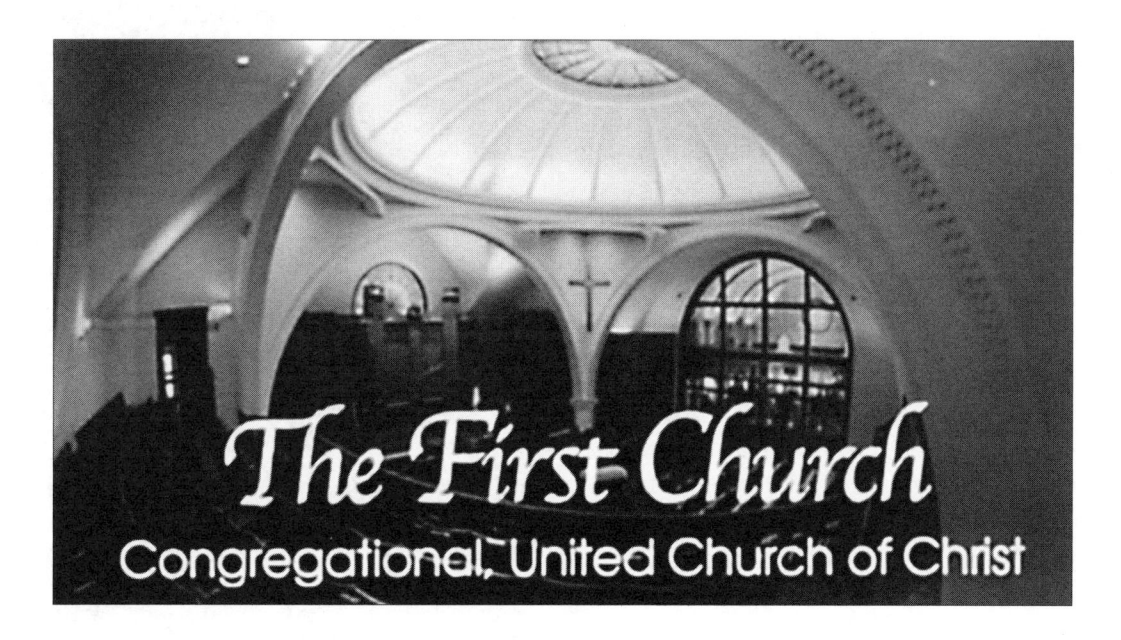

The Raising of Circus Tents

Roland Lesieur reminisces, "My great-uncle Dr. Oswald Maynard is the only person I ever knew who never sent out a bill. He lived next door to St. Joseph's and treated all the nuns, as well as the children in the orphanage. I lived through three big disasters: the 1930 Crown Hill fire, the 1936 flood (after Mass at St. Francis Xavier we saw three or four feet of water on Canal Street), and a 1938 hurricane (an amazing storm with trees down and no school for a week). On Saturdays we'd go to the Tremont to see the serials, mostly cowboy movies. I went on school fieldtrips to Benson's Animal Farm and rode the elephants. Once a circus came to town; elephants hauled tents up Hollis Street to the Fairgrounds. Nashua has wonderful memories."

TWO

THE ASSISTORS

"I note the obvious differences between each sort and type, but we are more alike, my friends, than we are unalike."

Maya Angelou
"Human Family"

The Chandler, a Victorian home to a former Nashua mayor, was deeded to the Nashua Public Library Board of Trustees upon his daughter Mabel's death in 1959. Her will stated, "This real property is to be used as a public library and shall be known as 'The Chandler Memorial Library' in memory of my family and me." The house was renovated, library furnishings were installed, and the dedication occurred in 1960. It remained a library until its closing in 2006.

Activist Carl Amelio received the Greater Nashua Chamber of Commerce's 1994 Citizen of the Year. In1963 Amelio coordinated efforts to make Nashua the FAA Boston Air Route Traffic Control Center. Uniting St. Joseph's Hospital and Rivier College, he established a bachelor's degree program for nursing and then evolved this into Rivier's Undergraduate Evening School. Amelio served the Community Council, Health Planning Council, St. Joseph's Community Services, Red Cross, and Boys Club.

In 1978 attorney David Gottesman founded Gottesman and Hollis, P.A. with attorney Morgan Hollis. New Hampshire Trials Lawyers Association recognized Gottesman in 2003 for establishing Internet privacy standards and for pro bono efforts supporting a New Hampshire man killed on 9/11/2001. Gottesman and Hollis were selected by their peers for The Best Lawyers In America annual list. Gottesman has served on community organizations and is a second term State Senator.

John "Jack" Berrigan has practiced law for thirty years with McLaughlin and Berrigan. He is past president of the Nashua Bar Association and remembers many cases where individual's testimonies played significant roles in the outcome of cases. His youngest son Jason and he live together, and Berrigan enjoys Thursday lunches with good friends, adding, "All in all, it's been a good trip, many more ups than downs, through life."

"I am so glad I was born and brought up in Nashua. It's been a great place to live," says Lucille "Lucy" Cudhea. Working for the Archie Slawsby Company, she became interested in the growth and changes in the city. Active in many political campaigns on the state and national levels, Lucy also served on various committees including the Arthritis Foundation, March of Dimes, and Good Cheer Society.

LOG CABIN INFORMATION BOOTH, NASHUA, N. H.

Two groups currently involved in promoting Nashua are the Greater Nashua Chamber of Commerce and the Great American Downtown (G.A.D.). Pictured above is an early Greater Nashua Chamber of Commerce information booth. Suzanne Butler is the executive director of G.A.D. Scott Cote is the Nashua president of G.A.D., an organization established "to develop and implement programs, projects, and events that positively shape the downtown experience." Says Butler, "I think Nashua has a lot going for it - great restaurants, shopping, history, arts and culture, and quality of life. It is a great place to raise a family, work and play."

Research engineer and engineering consultant Fred Teeboom settled his family in Nashua in 1972. In 1992 he joined the Taxpayers Association to learn how services, particularly education, are funded. Hoping to find better ways to influence budget decisions, he conducted independent research into limiting spending. Teeboom was one of the authors of the city's spending cap, an Alderman-At-Large, and creator of a forum allowing the public to speak at Aldermanic Board meetings.

O riginally from Nashua, Mary Doyle Keefe was Norman Rockwell's model for Rosie the Riveter, representative of women who entered the workforce to fill male jobs vacated by those who had gone off to fight in WWII. Mary was nineteen and paid $5.00 a day. Rockwell transformed her slim figure into Rosie's overly muscular physique. "Oh, there was lots of kidding and teasing"…but "hey, I sat for Rockwell," said Keefe.

Another young woman making a name for herself is Natalie Carr, a 2007 Nashua High School North graduate, who has been accepted by AmeriCorps, a service-based organization created in 1993. "I wanted to see what else was out there…There are lots of options." She will enter the National Civilian Corps division as a volunteer, doing service projects and responding to local and national disasters. At the end of service she will receive a scholarship. Carr's plans include college after AmeriCorps.

Rosie the Riveter

In the late 1800s – early 1900s Emile Chagnon Sr., "lumber king of the north," was manager of Chagnon and Sons Building Company which was known for constructing family dwellings and the original St. Joseph's Hospital. In 1914 he started Chagnon Lumber Company. Railroad cars unloaded inside the huge East Hollis Street building. At its peak the company had fourteen Mack trucks working twenty-four hours a day, six days a week. After the 1929 crash the company contracted to build houses. During WWII the company began to grow. Returning from the Air Force, Emile Jr., "Chag", helped expand the company, purchasing forklifts and a Temple Street freight house. After a 1983 fire the company rebuilt with the help of Emile's sons, Emille III (Brit) and Charles Edward. The lumber business closed in 1994 retaining the real estate and the brothers became commercial property owners.

Train heading south; train station in background.

Mabel Chandler's words reflect her life: "There is present reward in every worthy action. How important it is then, that we sow the seeds of purity, industry, and charity, that we live more for others than for ourselves. Human hearts grow rich and happy in daily rounds of usefulness and philanthropy." Mabel, businessman-politician Seth Chandler's daughter, bequeathed her home as a library. It closed in 2006. Another woman known for her charitable work was activist Isabelle Hildreth. She was associated with many local agencies and organizations that advanced social and civic causes especially for children, namely the Boys Club, *Telegraph*'s Santa Fund, Greater Nashua Child Care Center, Head Start, Red Cross, Nashua Heart Association, and Salvation Army. Hildreth was the first woman on the State Supreme Court's committee on Judicial Conduct.

June Caron was honored with the dedication and naming of the renovated park on Cottage and Temple streets as the June Caron Park. Caron began as a supervisor for the Nashua Parks and Recreation Department. In 1986 three parks commissioners were designated, marking the beginning of this department. Before then, none was needed. There were only two areas, North and South Commons, requiring summer hay cutting, tree planting, and walkway maintenance.

Le Parc de Notre Renaissance Francaise

Moving to Nashua in 1974, David Deane has been elected to the Board of Public Works and an Alderman-At-Large. He is best known for his care and concern for youth sports and has been president of North Youth Baseball and Babe Ruth Baseball. Deane worked with a group of young people to raise funding to construct a state of the art concrete skateboard park on Bridge Street.

Margaret Flynn came to Nashua in 1950 and partnered with her husband at Early & Flynn Law Offices. Her life is really that of an activist in social and civic causes. She was not only elected by Nashuans to the Board of Education, her peers made her president at a time many women crashed into the "glass ceiling." Serving as both a Director and a Trustee for Rivier College, Flynn still devoted her energy and time to the Nashua Police Commission, which was also groundbreaking for her gender. In 1986 she was appointed Justice of the New Hampshire Superior Court. Awards such as the Greater Nashua Chamber of Commerce Citizen of the Year, the Charitable Foundation Humanitarian winner, and the YMCA distinguished woman leader followed.

Nashua Police Station

Debora Pignatelli, Nashua resident since 1973, was the first Executive Director of the Nashua Girls Club. Holding office since 1986 as state representative then state senator, Pignatelli was elected to the Executive (Governor's) Council in 2004. She has been designated as one of the ten most powerful women in New Hampshire. "I believe people in public office must listen to all views and then vote with common sense and mainstream American principles in mind."

Nashua has an active Boys & Girls Club; in the 21st century they have joined forces in a renovated and expanded facility. There has long been established an organization call Girls Inc. which has been in existence throughout New England since the Industrial Revolution. Forward thinking women realized the need for their daughters to learn something that will earn them a living. Located at the Nashua Girls Center, this organization states, "It is our mission and passion to help girls achieve their personal best through a wide range of enrichment programs."

THE ASSISTORS

Adam Gureckis Sr. is a life-long resident of the Crown Hill area. He is a retiree of Nashua Corporation and a founding partner of WDER radio in nearby Derry, NH. Early on, Nashuans noticed his willingness to serve the community and elected him to several offices, including the New Hampshire House of Representatives and the Nashua Board of Aldermen. For many years now he has overseen the growth of the Triangle Credit Union from its days on Franklin Street to a financial institution with regional branches and impact. Gureckis' caring for his fellow man is best exemplified by his quarter century-plus as a director and a member of Harbor Homes. At the time of honoring his advocacy, CEO Peter Kelleher stated, "Because of Adam's passion, Harbor Homes is a stronger, more compassionate agency."

Triangle Credit Union

Harbor Homes

The law firm of Hamblett and Kerrigan was established by Charles Hamblett in 1889. The firm is located today in the three-story brick building on the corner of Main and Temple streets. David Hamblett not only served as full partner but also invested in other Nashua institutions, providing leadership to the *Nashua Telegraph* when the paper was a six afternoon-per-week journal. Attorney Joseph Kerrigan provided leadership in civic organizations. He has also successfully argued a case before the U.S. Supreme Court. "Their (our clients) problems and needs are our problems and needs. We communicate, we work hard, we care, and we do the job. It is a wonderful way to spend life and I am proud to be a part of it."— Kerrigan

Lester F. Thurber was an officer of the Second National Bank which began in 1875 in the Merchant's Exchange. Davis Thurber, his grandson, was also an officer of the bank for a number of years. He and his wife Patricia reside in Nashua. Both were involved in the forming of the Historic District. Their participation in the cultural community is evident by their support of the arts, especially contemporary art.

Second National Bank

Nashua native Aaron Harkaway, in private practice as an attorney for many years, was appointed Chief Justice of the Nashua District Court. He was a co-author of the state's Child Protection Act. Active in both civic affairs and civil rights, Harkaway was a member of the Beth Abraham Synagogue, the Nashua Zionist District, and the New Hampshire Zionist Federation. Ada, his wife, was office manager of her husband's law firm until his appointment as Chief Justice. Appearing regularly on the local weekly radio program "Impact," Mrs. Harkaway was also active in local and state politics as well as civic affairs including the Lawyers' Wives' Association, Nashua Symphony Women's Association, and Hadassah.

After graduation Nashua native Hugh Gregg founded Sullivan & Gregg Law firm. As alderman he helped bring in new area businesses. At thirty-two he became Mayor. His administration modernized the Publics Works Department and fully equipped the Police Station, consolidating law enforcement resources in the basement of City Hall at 229 Main Street, a W.P.A. project. Hugh Gregg went on to become the youngest New Hampshire Governor up to that point in time. His own political ambitions took second stage behind the family farm and businesses, but Gregg's efforts included the protecting of New Hampshire's presidential primary status, establishing the New Hampshire Political Library, and founding the Amos Tuck Society. Gregg was a supporter of the Humane Society, benefactor to the Crotched Mountain Rehabilitation Center, and a freelance writer. This foundation of public service has been carried on by his son Judd. Nashua and Hollis gave enough votes to the younger Gregg to gain the District Five Executive Council seat in the early 1970s. The nation knows Judd Gregg as a multi-term Governor, U.S. Congressman, and presently, United States Senator.

Hugh Gregg – center; Richard Nixon – right

The Assistors

Mrs. Mary H. and Miss Mary E. Hunt, in memory of husband and father Postmaster John Hunt, provided funds for two Nashua buildings. The Hunt Home for the Aged was dedicated in 1899. Previously in 1892 the Hunts had given a $50,000 gift to the city to erect a library. There was much discussion of a site. After court action the city took the Greeley lot on Railroad Square in 1895. The Hunt Memorial Library was completed in 1903. The clock was purchased by public subscription. Designed by New Hampshire native Ralph Adams Cram, the Hunt was used as administrative offices of the school department upon completion of the new library on Court Street in 1971. Since then the Hunt has been on the National Register of Historic Places. It is owned by the city and managed by an appointed board of trustees. Today many activities are held in its rooms including art exhibits, recitals, weddings, and even a visit from Mr. & Mrs. Claus.

Meri Goyette as Mrs. Claus *Ed Lecius, Jr. as Santa*

From mill workers to shop owners, many immigrants have settled in and called Nashua home. Their contributions to the community have been important, and examples of their culture remain. These families, regardless of ethnicity, possessed a tenacious work ethic. As one young descendant wrote, "My papou," Greek for grandfather, "has taught me you need to believe in yourself, work hard, and have passion to survive in this life." George and Bessie Tsiaras' lives are just two of the thousands of proud immigrant stories. Arriving from Greece and entering the United States through Ellis Island, the family, virtually penniless, settled in Nashua. Like many immigrant families, failure was not an option. Through hard work their four sons became respected and successful. Whether Greek, French, Irish, Jewish, or the many other ethnic groups which arrived, Nashua has been the grateful recipient of their many contributions.

George Scontsas and Ethel Scontsas

Ed Lecius, Jr. as Santa, Meri Goyette as Mrs. Claus (center photo)
Some of the holiday helpers, clockwise from top right: Dr. Charles Goyette, Timothy Glenday, George DeDousis, Ken Gidge, Fred Teeboom, Dr. Robert Moheban, _____ , John "Jack" Berrigan, Frank Teas Sr., David Rootovich, Tom Kelley

Tom Kelley not only held the position of Alderman-At-Large in the city but also the position of dean of the Nashua Board of Aldermen. No person has served as many terms as President of the Board as Mr. Kelley. Kelley Square, located at the intersection of Manchester Street and Henri Burque Highway, has been named in his honor. (Note Kelley's picture as one of the Salvation Army Bellringers.)

Tom Kelley

Thomas J. Leonard Sr. opened a law practice in Nashua in 1915. As a trial lawyer he represented people who didn't have a voice in government or law. He was active in the community organizing baseball and football games and was an early member of the country club. Two of his three sons, Thomas James Jr. and Richard Wilson, joined the law practice and were active in politics. Richard Wilson laid the cornerstone of the now Elm Street Middle School. William Leonard and his two brothers played on their college golf teams. Leonard Sr. was state amateur golf champ; Leonard Jr. and Richard won many golf championships. The law practice expanded in the late 1960s and early 1970s when lawyers Gerald Prunier, David Prolman, William Barry, William Groff, Jeffrey Mazerolle, and Steven Frasca joined the firm. In 1979 Thomas's son, Thomas J. Leonard III (known as Jay), joined the law firm.

Nashua Country Club

Nashua native Donnalee Lozeau was elected the 55th mayor of Nashua. Her public service career began as state representative from Nashua Ward 5. Throughout the years she has been active in numerous community organizations. In 1998 Mayor Lozeau was named to *New Hampshire Magazine*'s 10 Most Powerful Women. "I believe in the power of public service. Our community's single greatest asset is the people who live and work here."

Henri Burque was a lawyer, a mayor of Nashua, a Superior Court Judge of New Hampshire, and a justice of the State Supreme Court. A two-mile highway, connecting the old Boston to Concord U.S. Route 3 with the "Nashua By-Pass" is named the Henri A. Burque Highway in his honor. This highway is one of the few surface roads maintained year round by the state of New Hampshire because it connects federal and state routes.

Trolley, an early form of city transportation.

Warren Rudman, United States Senator, attended Nashua public school, graduated from the Boston College of Law, admitted to the New Hampshire Bar in 1960, and began practicing in Nashua. He has held many political positions both statewide and on the federal level. His highest elected post was the aforementioned multi-terms in the U.S. Senate. Here in New Hampshire he served as Attorney General. As a senator he served as the chairman of the Select Committee on Ethics. President Clinton appointed him a member of the Foreign Intelligence Advisory Board. He has served as co-chair of the US committee on National Security. Rudman has often taken on the difficult investigations our country has needed, such as Iran/Contra. Rudman is also co-founder of the Concord Coalition, and, not far from his longtime Indian Rock Road home, the establishment of Daniel Webster College, which began in 1965 at Boire Field as the New England Aeronautical Institute. Today it is a full, four-year college.

Daniel Webster Hall at Daniel Webster College

Daniel Webster College Aviation Center

William Roby Swart, son of Colonel William D. Swart, served on several local boards, was a longtime treasurer of the *Telegraph*, and with his wife Margaret Beasom Swart, founded the former Arts and Science Center. Opening in the 1960s on East Pearl Street, the Center moved into a three-level building on Court Street in 1973. The space included a renovated section of the old Central Fire Station. That station, dedicated in 1871 and originally manned by citizen firemen, was described as "modern with a tendency towards the Gothic style of architecture in the construction and finish of the gables and towers." There was also an expansive addition to house a meeting room, theater, art galleries, children's museum, and facilities for workshops, courses, and studios for dance, painting and sculpture. There also is a mural in the lobby depicting Nashua scenes commissioned by Margaret Swart.

The old Central Fire Station, Court Street

City Hall Steeple

City Hall Eagle

By the mid 1960s, Dennis J. Sullivan was known as the postmaster of Nashua. Mr. Sullivan then became the next Mayor of Nashua. He would be elected every two years for the next decade; only ill health ended his political career in 1977. Mayor Sullivan was on board as Nashua built a new senior high school, a new public library, installed improved downtown street lighting, and implemented parallel parking in the business district. Mayor Sullivan did have an unsuccessful run as a Democrat for the post of Governor of New Hampshire. A federally funded ninety-six unit highrise apartment building for the elderly was opened on Tyler Street in 1970 and named Sullivan Terrace in honor of the former mayor.

THE ASSISTORS

In 1957 Mario Vagge was elected Nashua's first full-time mayor, the first of his four terms. Life member of the Nashua's Lions Club and named Greater Nashua Chamber of Commerce "Man of the Year," he was involved in many organizations: Knights of Columbus, Boy Scouts, Crotched Mountain Rehabilitation Center, Friendship Club, and Little League (which he helped found). Vagge was a trustee of Daniel Webster College. The state's first low-income, elderly housing project was named Vagge Village. Other Nashua mayors were Milton Taylor, Jeremiah Doyle, Andros Jones, Albert Shedd, William Barry, James Crowley, Henri Burque, Eaton Sargent, William Sullivan, Alvin Lucier, Frank McMaster, Eugene Lemay, Oswald Maynard, Hugh Gregg, Claude Nichols, Lester Burnham, Mario Vagge, Dennis Sullivan, Donald Davidson, Maurice Arel, Thomas Leonard III, James Donchess, Rob Wagner, Donald Davidson, Bernard Streeter, and Donnalee Lozeau.

120 Main Street
City Hall (1843–1940) and Municipal Records Building (1866–1940)

229 Main Street
New City Hall (dedicated in 1938)

Because Nashua is a physically large city, in excess of thirty square miles, the neighborhoods each needed to have retail services within them. The history of the neighborhood markets of this city reveals colorful distinctions of the items for sale and the methods to provide service. Champagne's on East Hollis Street was the home of S&H green stamps and famous meat cutter Al Cote. In northwest Nashua Arthur Jean and sons provided residents with Foodland, a place where one could leave the wallet at home and put tonight's dinner fixings "on account." Soucy's Market had homegrown produce and hired kids to deliver orders. Liamos Market still is the home to cuts of lamb plus the ability to have the daily newspaper saved for you at the cash register.

The Assistors

Left to right, top to bottom: Bernie Streeter, Beth McCarthy, Father Alexopoulos, Frank Mooney; John Malkowski with his mother Lillian, Jay Dinkle Jr., Robin Luna, Carole Murphy; Neil Koppenhaver, Carolyn Choate and Don Marquis, Marty Capodice, Meri Goyette and Donald Davidson.

Pharmacist Bradley Whitney remembers his childhood. "I grew up in rural South Nashua during the Great Depression when bare essentials were all that anyone had. We never went to a restaurant. We put our trash in a barrel and burned it on rainy days. Once a week we put a bucket out with garbage for a farmer to feed his pigs. We walked a mile to school and back twice a day. We had an iceman, a bread man, a milkman, and the grocer delivered our order to our house. At twelve I operated my popcorn cart on East Hollis Street at the Hudson Bridge during the summer. Benson's Animal Farm customers were my mainstay. At sixteen I owned the New Hampshire dealership for Whizzer Motor Bikes, selling them out of the abandoned World War II enemy-airplane lookout shack built on our property."

A ride at Benson's Wild Animal Farm

THREE

THE COMMUNICATORS

"Men come and go, some leave a trace
Of efforts through the years,
A memory perhaps of joy,
A distant thought of tears."

B. Telfair Mines
"The Stone Wall"

The Communicators

The Webster dictionary defines communication as the giving or interchanging of thoughts, feelings, information or the like by writing, speaking, etc. For 175 years *The Telegraph* has been the area's prominent print source with local, national, and international news as well as sports, feature articles, supplements, and special editions. In 1832 the paper was a weekly known as *The New Hampshire Telegraph*; in 1869 it became *The Nashua Daily Telegraph*. After occupying space in the city for many years, the newspaper moved to larger quarters in Hudson, New Hampshire.

For over two decades Arnie Arnesen has been involved in New Hampshire politics and the media. Arnesen says, "Political candidates have a choice…they can either pander to people's fears in an effort to win or speak the truth in an effort to lead." She has had a bi-weekly column in the *Boston Globe* and is a regular speaker at major academic institutions. Today people can enjoy her self-produced program "Political Chowder" on both radio and television.

Librarian and historian Florence Shepard is credited with two works of local history: as editor of *The Nashua Experience* (1978) and as author of *Nashua, New Hampshire: a pictorial history* (1989). In 1988 Ms. Shepard was named the first recipient of the Mayor's Award for Superior Achievement in Arts and Letters.

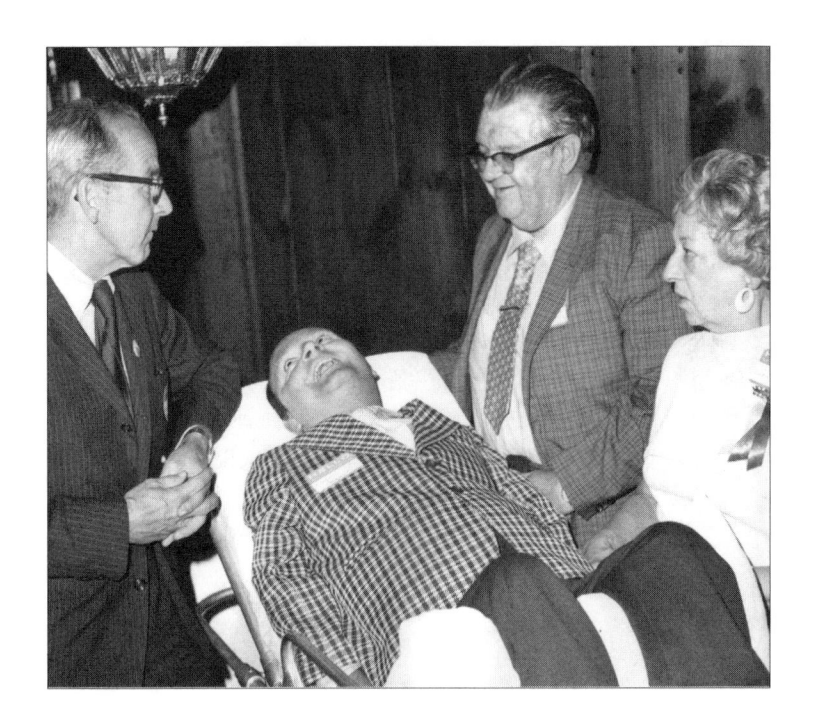

Not to Doubt and *All I Can Give* recounted Richard "Dickie" Chaput's life affected by polio which had paralyzed him at nine from the neck down. As an adult, Chaput was president of the Friendship Club. In 1954 the Friendship Club opened, a gathering place for area men and women who have physical disabilities. He was an officer of the Gate City Chapter of the National Association of the Physically Handicapped (founded by friend Marilyn Woods) and an inspirational lecturer managing over one hundred speaking engagements a year. In 1966 the National Jaycees honored Chaput as one of ten outstanding young men.

The Friendship Club, Orchard Heights

Telegraph reporter and editor Frederick Dobens was known for his news sense and trademark pipe. He began in 1923 by writing general news stories. His column was "F.H.D.'s Around the Town." Dobens was also active in community and civic service affairs including the Greater Nashua Chamber of Commerce, City Park & Recreation Commissioner, and Chairman of the Hunt Library trustees. By 1948 he was the paper's managing editor.

Frank Teas Sr. began working for radio station WSMN in 1958 as an announcer and program manager. He became an account executive for the station and the *1590 Broadcaster* that came along six years later. Frank Teas Day was proclaimed in 1993 by the governor of New Hampshire and Nashua Mayor Wagner in honor of his commitment to community service. Frank reads the news to his fellow Rotarian members at weekly luncheons. His son, G. Frank Teas, is President and CEO of the Nashua Bank on Main Street.

Frank Teas Sr.

G. Frank Teas

The Communicators

Ed Lecius, Jr.

Broadcaster Edward F. Lecius, Sr. was Nashua's first electronic newsman, starting his live broadcasts from the news events of the gate city in the late 1940s. Mr. Lecius joined the news radio station WSMN when it signed on in the late 1950s. While Ed broadcasted the news and sports, his brother Peter joined the sales team, which added a weekly paper to the fold in 1964. Ed Lecius, Sr. was joined by his son Edward, using the name Lee Edwards to avoid confusion, to broadcast sports to Nashua High School fans in the early 1970s. A civic leader in his own right, Ed Lecius, Jr. comments on Talk Radio: "People do want to know. Talk radio gives an opportunity to delve into local interests. Politics? People do not respect the sanctity of confidential matters." Lecius, Jr. is also an international Lions Club Director who has served at the U.S. Department of Commerce and at FEMA. Says Ed, "In Nashua we have an all-hands approach." Both Ed Lecius, Sr. and Jr. began their Holman Stadium broadcasts with the promise to be the listeners "Eye in the Sky."

A football broadcast from Holman Stadium

Jeannine T. Levesque, a second generation Nashua native, was employed at *The Telegraph*, and later the public library as a community services coordinator and reference librarian. She pursued her interest in local history contributing a poem, "To Our Ancestors," to a book published in conjunction with the dedication of Le Parc de Notre Renaissance Francaise. Ms. Levesque is also writing a history of the Infant Jesus Church, founded in 1909.

At Rivier College Sharron Rowlett was invited to develop and administer a new Office of Multicultural Affairs in 1997. A graduate and undergraduate adjunct faculty member, she has brought to campus "The Artifacts of Slavery," an exhibit documenting the transatlantic slave trade. Rowlett has served on many committees and panels. Rowlett says, "History helps us to understand where we were yesterday, where we are today, and how to get there tomorrow."

In 1871, Union Atheneum, a private reading club, had been formed and agreed to donate its entire holdings if the city supported a public library. In 1867, the Nashua Public Library was established as a tax-supported, free institution first located in an unused section of the second floor of the new County Records Building erected next to City Hall. By 1903 when the Hunt Memorial Library had opened, there was a Children's Room in the back wing. Later the Children's Department was located downstairs. A mural with New Hampshire wildflowers covered the walls. Among the librarians was Clara Smith, assistant librarian (1916), who believed that the library belonged to all of the people. Forrest B. Spaulding (1917-19) was elected head librarian upon Miss Smith's retirement. Rachel Sanborn was a reference librarian. Elizabeth Spring, Children's Librarian, was one of the writers of *The Nashua Experience* and author of *Obadiah Comes 14*, a young people's book about Nashua history. Florence Shepard retired after twenty-eight years service to the library.

The former Circulation Desk

Children's room at the former Nashua Public Library

Abbot-Spalding House

When Miss Sylvia Spalding, the last surviving member of the family who had owned the 1802 Daniel Abbot home, died in 1984, the Nashua Historical Society began transforming the house into a museum. Originally in 1802 Daniel Abbot, referred to as the "father of Nashua," had purchased the home from John Lund with the lawn extending to the Sailors and Soldiers Monument. Abbot was a lifelong friend of Daniel Webster and Franklin Pierce. Eventually General William Spalding bought the home in 1905. Upon his death in 1922, the house was inherited by a son and daughter. Today the eight-room house, with its donated contents, is on the National Register of Historic Places and the New Hampshire State Register of Historic Places. The home is open during the summer months, keeping with a request that the facility be used as a museum and teaching resource for the community.

Florence H. Speare Memorial Museum
Home of The Nashua Historical Society

Thomas and Athais Dube *Louis and Melina Noel*

GRANDPARENTS OF PAULINE NOEL MOONEY

Curator Beth McCarthy is responsible for the care, preservation, and management of the Nashua Historical Society's collection. Engineer Frank Mellen, longtime member, has been active in city and church groups. Postal Carrier Frank Mooney, a Nashua High School graduate and also a member, is known for his membership and volunteer spirit at other civic organizations. The Nashua Historical Society was organized in 1870 to preserve the past for the future. At first, meetings were held at members' homes. After land was acquired on Abbott Street and through a trust set up by Sceva Speare, a Main Street merchant, in honor of his deceased wife, a new fireproof building known as the Florence Hyde Speare Memorial Museum was constructed with the dedication in 1972. In 1978 the Society purchased the federal revival Abbot-Spalding House which contains fine furnishings.

Writer Stacie Milbouer's journalism career has been with the *Boston Globe*, *Union Leader*, and *The Telegraph*. She has published short stories and poems and is the co-author of *Dying in Vein: Blood Deception…Justice*. Stacie's awards include New Hampshire Press Association's Writer of the Year and Columnist of the Year. Stacie is currently responsible for the Internet website "Doorbell Gourmet" and she is a teacher at the Nackey Loeb School of Communication.

The Telegraph Building in right foreground

Except for a non-newspaper job after college, Marilyn Solomon has always worked in print. Joining *The Telegraph*'s editorial staff in 1978, she founded Culinary Delights, a cooking contest. She ran the newly-created Nashua bureau in the 1990s until her retirement in 2002. Ms. Solomon authored *My Window on Main Street*, a series of anecdotes that portray life in Nashua.

Rose Arthur, program founder and director of R.I.S.E. (Rivier Institute for Senior Education), researched the idea and then held an open house in 1997 which attracted 100 people. The curriculum with a motto of "RISE is a program where curiosity never retires" has continued to grow with courses led by experts and enthusiasts and the availability of the campus at Rivier College. Rivier College was named in honor of the Blessed Anne Marie Rivier, foundress of the Sisters of Presentation of Mary. Established first in 1933 in Hudson, New Hampshire, the campus moved in 1941 to its present Nashua campus. The core mission of that Catholic institution is "dedicated to transforming hearts and minds to serve the world." The fully-accredited college is invested with the power to confer both undergraduate and graduate degrees in liberal arts and professional courses.

Barbara Pressly has been known as a public servant, an activist, and in her words "a consumer advocate." She was a supporter of the commuter rail and filed as an intervener in the city's case to purchase the Pennichuck Water Corp. before the Public Utilities Commission. Active in city government, as well as serving two terms in both the House of Representatives and State Senate, Pressly was also charter chairperson of the city Historic District Commission.

Edmund Keefe began teaching U.S. History and Ancient History at Nashua High School on Spring Street in 1929. He was the school principal by 1945, appointed Superintendent of Schools in 1958, and retired in 1973. Keefe was a member of the Nashua Historical Society who created the fourth-grade tours as part of local history studies. He served eight terms as state representative from Ward 8. Keefe Auditorium is named for him.

The former Nashua High School, Spring Street

Penny Geer, an Amherst Street Elementary School teacher, is remembered by her colleagues. "She embodies the spirit of the school probably more than anyone else. I think we were all fortunate for having her around. She gave so much of herself to the school. She wanted to do things that would benefit children. Everyone that had the privilege of knowing her will carry on that spirit."

The original Amherst Street Elementary School

Social liberal and activist Joseph Sakey came to the Hunt Memorial Library in 1956. Under Sakey's leadership the Bookmobile and Chandler Library were added to the Nashua library system. Art and music collections, the Business Library, and Great Books Discussion groups are just a few of the services that became realities under Sakey. He is known for persisting in the struggle for a new library. Meanwhile in community affairs, Sakey was a founding member of the new Symphony Orchestra and the Arts & Science Center. Owner of a local radio station, Sakey became involved with numerous commissions and boards. His wife Shirley assisted her husband in many of his endeavors and was active politically in the League of Women Voters. The husband and wife team manned the polls every election day at the Amherst Street School for many years.

Dean and Michael Shalhoup

Michael Shalhoup joined *The Telegraph* in 1952 as photographer, sports writer, and general reporter, later becoming the regional editor, then city editor, and finally the managing editor until his retirement in 1985. In 1992 Shalhoup wrote a series on area athletes, as well as for the special edition celebrating Nashua's sesquicentennial. His historic photographs have been seen in Associated Press dispatches of events, in books, and in community exhibits. In 1972 Dean Shalhoup, Michael's son, began at *The Telegraph* as newsroom assistant, sports writer, photographer, and darkroom operator. He was named sports editor in 1976, staff photographer in 1979, and then chief photographer. In 2001 Dean became the community's feature writer. Dean also writes a weekly column about Nashua's past and serves on the boards of both the Nashua Historical Society and the Greater Nashua Salvation Army.

From a student who wrote, "You are the best teacher I have had" to an administrator who said of his daughter's "wonderful experience in your classroom," Stanley Stoncius is recognized not only as a teacher and administrator but also one who has devoted a great deal to preserving the local Lithuanian heritage. Each year the Gate City enjoys musical selections and religious services provided by ongoing fundraising and networking conducted by Stoncius.

Matthew Matsis, lifetime educator for thirty-seven years, worked in the Nashua School District first as a teacher then as an assistant principal. He applied many school principles as a tennis chair umpire or as a line judge twice for the U.S. Open and once for the Australian Open. Matsis said he always valued his time as an educator. "My main concentration was the kids. Tennis came second."

Don Marquis remembers "an amazing social studies department" filled with special teachers. He held the position first as a teacher then as department coordinator. Realizing the tremendous public interest in local history, he conducted downtown walking tours "that were so much fun" to the Hunt, the Millyard, and various churches. Attendance was overwhelming. Marquis served on the Hunt Board of Trustees during a time where the main objective was to restore the 1903 Hunt building to its past glory. After many years of neglect and vacancy, the building was reopened for entertainment, enlightenment, and the company of friends. Marquis and Meri Goyette promoted this renovation both in print and on local television. On leaving the school district Marquis developed and conducted workshops on how to use primary sources in the classroom for teachers of gifted and talented students. This required many cross country flights to the Los Angeles, California school district.

Don and Mary "Shaun" Marquis

Nashua High School, now Elm Street Middle School

One-room schoolhouse, South Nashua

An 1853 law made age five the requirement for entering Nashua schools. Discipline and Academic Achievement reports were issued. In the 1870s, high school students paid tuition and, like grade school pupils, bought their own books and supplies. By 1873 evening classes were offered for boys and girls who worked in the mills. In 1885 drawing and physical pursuits were added to the curriculum. The first kindergarten opened in 1893 and, although for many years there were private, public, and parochial schools, no private elementary schools opened until 1883. Schools were never shut because of bad weather though closing occurred because of smallpox and scarlet fever. Records show many made teaching a career. In the 1890s a Teachers' Club was formed to promote teaching power and general culture.

People from surrounding towns have flocked to join Nashuans for various parades and celebrations with many ceremonies held on the steps of City Hall. In 1876 the Centennial Celebration of the Declaration of Independence included sports events and fireworks. Torchlight parades were common the month before presidential elections. In 1922 a lengthy parade recognized the 200 mile Daniel Webster Highway with a ceremony at the state line where two granite markers were unveiled. A three-day celebration with a carnival show and bonfire was held in 1928 for the city's seventy-fifth anniversary. Many annual parades began to be known for their costumes and floats about that time. The city's 1953 Centennial Parade featured the "Mummers" from Philadelphia, who returned a year later to fund-raise for the Centennial Swimming Pool. The nation's Bicentennial Parade was the result of planning years earlier by a local committee. Annually there are parades commemorating Memorial and Veterans' Days.

International sculptors were chosen to create sculptures for the city's Sculpture Symposiums providing one form of public art free and accessible for all. Each piece is unique, but the human themes and perspectives communicated through the art are timeless. It would be impossible to speak of each sculptor who has contributed his share in this most inventive endeavor. John Weidman, co-founder of the Andres Institute of Art in Brookline, New Hampshire and Director of Nashua's Symposium, is a sculptor whose first work, "Monument to Memory" stands at the south entrance of Nashua. Other participating international sculptors included Luben Boykov, Vaclav Fiala, James Gagnon, Michele Golia, Tomas Oliva, Mae Thi Thu Van and Sara Mae Wasserstrum. Public art displays also include murals, sculptures, architecture and historic artifacts which can be seen in the city.

Monument to Memory
John Weidman, sculptor
Main Street rotary at Rivier College

The Taras Fountain
J.W. Fiske, manufacturer
Abbot-Spalding House and Grounds

Yankee Flyer Diner

Cynthia Kyriax Burney's memories are from the 1950s. "At Crowley School air raid drills were practiced by crouching and covering our heads. In the summer popcorn was sold from carts at the city's north and south ends. Millers offered teens an account to charge clothing. Speare's Dry Goods used little overhead trolleys to transport money to the accounts' department. Woolworth's 5 & 10 sold a variety of goods and had a food counter. At Christmastime, Main Street's First National Grocery Store sold 12" tall gingerbread men. A candy store on the corner of Elm and Lake streets was off-limits during school hours. Once my friend and I walked in the middle of the snowy two-way Kinsley Street to the Yankee Flyer Diner. (Spring Street Junior High School's annual Student Council luncheon was held there). And who could forget the narrow, connecting tunnel from that school to the Quincy Street Annex?"

FOUR

THE PROVIDERS

*"In every town and village, In every city square,
In crowded places I search the faces
Hoping to find Someone to care."*

Maya Angelou
"Where We Belong, A Duet"

Emergency Hospital, circa 1907

The early City Hospital

Prior to 1900 unsuitable apartments at the almshouse, the City Hall, and the police buildings cared for the poor and injured. Doctors appealed for relief because of the rising number of manufacturing accidents and therefore the Nashua Emergency Hospital Association was formed. A building was erected to accommodate medical and surgical cases. Today Nashua offers two modern hospital complexes, St. Joseph's and Southern New Hampshire Medical Center (formerly Memorial Hospital), as well as a number of medical support services such as Home Health and Hospice, nursing homes, Meals on Wheels, and Lifeline Response System.

In 1989 Senior Pastor Paul Berube, a Nashua native, and a group of believers from the Abbott Loop Christian Center in Anchorage, Alaska started Grace Fellowship Church. Various rented facilities in Nashua were used for services until the purchase of a building at 43 Main Street in 1989.

In 1995 The Greeley House on Front Street on the Nashua River was acquired by the Grace Fellowship Church for administrative offices, youth ministries, and a counseling center. The house, a last remnant of an out-of-the-way residential area, was built over 150 years ago by Joseph Greeley (not related to the others of the same name in Nashua) and can be seen from the Main Street bridge. It is now used for visiting speakers and missionaries. In 1997 the Franklin Mill Building was added to the campus. "Prayer is the 'ethos' of everything we do at Grace."

Countless young people have benefited from the Boys & Girls Club dedication "only to children—their character, their happiness, their hopes and opportunities for successful lives" and mission "to enable all young people …to reach their potential as productive, caring, responsible citizens." In 1971 the Boys Club (retrofitting to serve girls occurred in 1995) opened to 300 members from a rented storefront on Main Street. Don Norris was the first volunteer president. Dominick Giovinazzo, the club's first CEO, and the board raised money to build the current clubhouse on Grand Avenue in Nashua's inner-city in the early 1970s. An indoor swimming pool was added in 1975. In 1992 the board of directors created an endowment to help the club withstand financial changes and ensure stability. In 1999 Norm Bouthilette took over as CEO and in 2007 membership topped 4,200 children.

"He was a wonderful, caring doctor," said a former patient of Dr. Sidney Curelop, an internist and nephrologist. Curelop was a new breed of physician…the specialist (prior doctors had been general practitioners). Curelop established the first dialysis center at Memorial Hospital, created the hospital's first medical library and the first coronary intensive care unit, and founded a credentialing committee. Curelop remembers Dr. Buttrick: "With Bud, it was absolute devotion to the mission."

Dr. Wallace Buttrick practiced medicine for thirty-nine years. A member of the New Hampshire Medical Association, he also served on the Board of Registration in Medicine. Nashua recognized Dr. Buttrick for his volunteer time and expertise to the Public Health Department HIV AIDS Task Force.

Mary Caprio, a longtime Nashua resident, was first employed as a nurse in Pennsylvania, New Jersey, and Maryland. In Nashua she was a registered nurse and a nursing instructor at St. Joseph School of Nursing. She also assisted her husband Vito at his business, the former Carter's Men's Shop on Main Street. The Caprios donated to the hospital the Italian artist Verginer's sculpture of St. Joseph, patron saint of the hospital.

Verginer's Sculpture of St. Joseph

The Humane Society for Greater Nashua and Executive Director Karen Bill acknowledge many accomplishments of the staff and volunteers. The Humane Society, in a new building since 1978, also administers the Proctor Cemetery for Animals, started in the 1920s on the present Ferry Hill Road. The Society's collection boxes in the shape of little white houses with green roofs can be seen in various area establishments. Curley is pictured here with Doctor Charles Goyette.

Nashua is home to many faiths. A few are either mentioned here or elsewhere in this book. The Church of the Good Shepherd (pictured) is a regrouping from the Episcopalian First Church and St. Lukes. The Main Street Methodist Church is among the oldest buildings in Nashua. St. Louis de Gonzague of 1871, the city's second oldest Catholic parish, burned in 1976; the central tower was salvaged and incorporated into the new structure. The Greek community had two churches: in 1913 the Church of the Annunciation and in 1922 St. Nicholas. After years of separation both churches were sold and in 1973 merged into St. Philip Greek Orthodox and was built in the grove which had been the site of many church functions.

The Providers

Dr. Norman Crisp helped found St. Joseph's Trauma Center and served on the Board of Education. In the 1980s the elementary school on Arlington Street was named in his honor. The school abuts Gardner-Roussel Park, a public park. For more than a decade he was in practice with his two sons, surgeons Norman Crisp Jr. and John Crisp. Earlier in the practice of medicine in the city were two women doctors. Dr. Katherine Hoyt in 1888 opened a general practice office. In 1892 she devoted her time to gynecology-obstetrics. She was a New Hampshire Medical Society member. In 1888 Dr. Ellen Blaylock Atherton opened her practice to women and children. She was the Medical Society's first female member, one of the first doctors of the Emergency Hospital, and a founder of Memorial Hospital (Southern New Hampshire Medical Center).

Norman Crisp, Jr. M.D.

Former St. Joseph Hospital, Kinsley Street

Norman Hall presently owns and operates (with his son, funeral director Andrew) Davis Funeral Home. Norman has been with the home since 1972 and acquired the business in 1987. Of him it has been said, "A more compassionate person will never be found." The business was established in 1842 by a local gravestone maker named Davis. The undertaking business had become an accepted institution by the 1880s. Early records show complete services of ready-made coffins and mourning wakes. The hearse had a glass compartment into which the casket was placed. The horses were draped in black. The Davis Home is Nashua's oldest and the second oldest in the state. With its trademark candle and logo, "One Memory Lights Another," since 1995 the Davis Funeral Home has been the recipient of the Pursuit of Excellence Award by the National Funeral Directors Association.

*Aerial of Lock and Whitney streets
Davis Funeral Home – center*

Woodlawn Cemetery, Kinsley Street

Saint Christopher's School

In his twenties, Charley Glenday was named the principal of the new Alvirne High School in 1951. His summer job in the personnel department of Sanders Associates, Inc. became permanent in 1954. He left thirty years later as assistant to the president. During Glenday's many years as V.P. for Corporate Affairs, facilities were constructed from South Portland, ME to Plainview, NJ, and in greater Nashua. The people on these projects were solicited by Glenday to aide in the construction of the St. Christopher's School, the St. Patrick's Center, and the Parish of the Resurrection Hall on Broad Street. Glenday served on the Greater Nashua Chamber of Commerce, the Nashua Housing Authority, the Nashua Police Commission, the Alvirne Trustee Board, and along with Dr. Jack Crisp, as one of the first two civilians on the board at St. Joseph Hospital, overseeing the doubling in size of that institution.

Charles Goyette, MD delivered two generations of Nashua children. Son of a small-town physician, he built a medical practice in Nashua, joined by Doctors Normand Cote and Joseph "Fran" Duval as associates. *One Man's Story* is an autobiographical reflection of his life from boyhood to the practice of medicine. Devoted husband and loving father to his family of six children, Dr. Charlie's warmth for people touched thousands of former patients and friends.

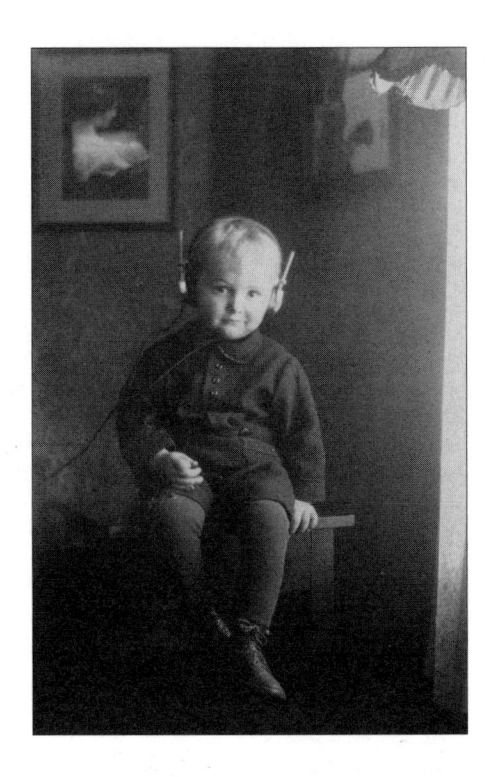

Charles Goyette

Doctor Robert Moheban was both Nashua hospitals' Department Chairman for Surgery and founder of the Nashua Ostomy Association. One of the Boys and Girls Club founders, he established a college scholarship endowment fund for club members. He was awarded the National Service to Youth Award for forty years' service. Moheban carried the 1996 Olympic torch to City Hall, to which a family member stated, "Dad can carry an Olympic torch without tripping, while being chased by helicopters and motorcades."

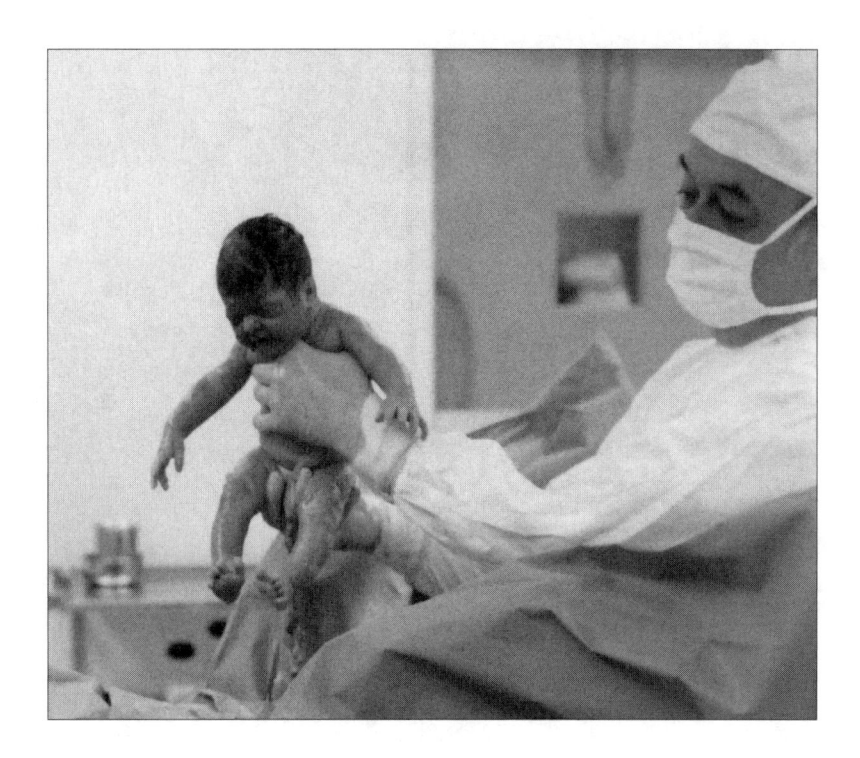

Dr. Charles Goyette

The year was 1955; young men and women, graduating from medical schools, were not willing to pursue a career as family doctor; more and more were turning towards special interests in medicine. A new breed of doctor was finding places in small cities. Dr. Charles Goyette, obstetrics and gynecology, opened his office in an old, brown-shingled building at 207 Main Street. Soon others followed: Dr. Sidney Curelop, internal medicine; and Dr. James Waugh, general surgeon. They were forerunners of other early specialists: Dr. Everett Tuttle, Dr. William Garvey, Dr. James Sullivan, and Dr. E. Thorpe—all pediatricians. The task confronting them was not an easy one. Nashuans were used to the family practitioner who treated all ailments. Why were specialists needed? Who were they whose medical practices covered only one specific part of the body? Medicine changed rapidly in the early years. Women were being accepted as highly-regarded physicians—rather unheard of in the early 20th century. It was a difficult time, but finally they were accepted; today the phonebook's Yellow Pages indicate these professionals are definitely part of the equation.

Salvation Army Band

Majors Donald and Priscilla Klemanski, retired after almost forty-five years of service to the Salvation Army, were honored for dedicated service through men's, women's, and children's programs. Major Barbara and Carl Carvill are now the Corps officers. Carvill is also the Nashua Fire Department Protestant Chaplain. The Salvation Army, inspiring with "soup, soap, and salvation" began in London in 1865. By the 1900s the Army had spread around the world and is now in 106 nations. Social services provided in Nashua include the food pantry, clothing room, referrals for assistance, back to school backpacks, holiday help with turkey dinners, clothing and toys, community care with luncheons for seniors, and emergency disaster services. Community services include the Learning Zone with after school and summer activities. Adventure Corps and Sunbeams which are Christian Education and emblem achievement programs are also offered.

George DeDousis and David D. "Doc" Cote

The Providers

Asked about his life and accomplishments, John Latvis assures all that it has been "peaches and cream" and "Thank you Nashua, and God Bless You All." With a 1938 Nashua High School diploma and a Harvard Business School degree, Latvis set up a training program for Textron and then began a career in the insurance field. He became Park Recreation Director, joined many organizations, and purchased the Clancy Building, remodeling it into a part of the Southern New Hampshire Medical Center. In 1980 Latvis and his wife Maida purchased the historic Stark House on Concord Street. (The 1853 Stark House was built for George Stark, grandson of the General John Stark, hero of Bennington in 1777. George Stark became Superintendent of the Lowell and Nashua Railroad. The home is of the Italian villa design with first floor windows with a double arch within and a balcony above. For many years it was owned by the Christian Science Church. The house is on the National Register of Historic Places and is now the location of Latvis Insurance and Real Estate).

Maida and John Latvis

Walkers, boaters, fishermen, cross-country skiers, and bikers enjoy Mine Falls, the 325 acre park of forest, wetlands, and open fields. Several fields are used for organized sports. The Nashua River borders Mine Falls to the north; to the south is Millpond and the Canal System. Mine Falls derives from the 1700s when low quality lead was supposedly mined from an island below the falls. In the 1800s workers with mules and shovels dug the three-mile canal. The first gates were built in 1826; the Gatehouse near the falls was built in 1886. In 1992 the trails of Mine Falls Park became part of the New Hampshire Heritage Trail System, a trail stretching across the state from the Massachusetts border to the Canadian border, over 200 miles long.

A friend with Meri Goyette on right

The Providers

The First Church was officially organized in 1685 and a burial ground adjacent to the church was laid out. Isaac Spalding's wife Lucy gave generously to the church. By 1894 the congregation moved into the granite building at the top of Library Hill, and the tall tower was raised. This site had originally been the old Indian Head Coffee House where stage coaches had once pulled up, and many social affairs had been held. Barbara Pressly served as Deaconess of the First Church of Nashua, creating equalization of women's roles in church service rituals.

The First Church

In 1892 a group of Jewish settlers had gathered for regular services. The first Nashua synagogue was constructed in 1899, modernization occurred in 1927, and the current Temple Beth Abraham was built in 1960.

The first Synagogue in Nashua

The Hebert family retained the name "Rice's Pharmacy" when they began operating the historic facility decades ago. Located on Main Street on the bridge overlooking the Nashua River, it is New Hampshire's oldest pharmacy, dating from 1868. Roger Hebert may have taken over the reigns as owner in 1995, but he was already a clerk at Rice's when he was twelve years old. Hebert had been named recipient of the Young Pharmacist Award by the state and is past president of the New Hampshire Pharmacists Association. He now heads a team of technicians, pharmacists, and delivery staff who provide compounding services and an array of medical supplies to greater Nashua.

In 1958 Reverend Donald Rowley became the Unitarian Universalist Church's minister. He helped develop White Wing Kindergarten. He founded Nashua's Mental Health Committee and chaired many others: Community Council's Mental Health Planning Association, Fair Housing Practices. Rowley served on the boards of Harbor Homes, Adult Learning Center, Big Brother, and advised New Hampshire-Vermont Blue Shield and Mathew Thornton HMO. In 1985 Rowley was presented with an Honorary Doctor of Divinity. He retired in 1987. The Unitarian Church, constructed in 1827 in the neo-classic design by architect Asher Benjamin, is the oldest church building in Nashua. Its huge, solid, front columns were felled trees from a nearby town. The church was moved twenty feet in 1929 when the parish house was built. The combined Unitarian-Universalist Church bought the burned-out Armory site on Canal Street in 1957 and added a Sunday school and office wing. The nearby Nashua Cemetery, started in 1835, is the burial site of many famous Nashuans including Daniel Abbot, the "Father of Nashua," and Major General John Foster, Civil War officer who has a statue in Foster Square.

Consumers have changed shopping habits from the independent small store to large shopping complexes. In 1963 builder Joseph Simoneau with his sons Paul, Norman, and Rene opened Simoneau Plaza at 300 Main Street. The Plaza, displaying a thirty-foot neon sign topped with a five-foot star, was sold in 1996. Grandson Alan continues to use the shape of the sign for his construction company's logo. The mall developed problems with ground settling causing sloping floors in stores. This resulted because the site was on the 1940s filled Harbor Pond which was part of the Salmon Brook system. The American Shearing Company plant was torn down in 1972 when the plaza expanded. The Pheasant Lane Mall, opened in 1986, was partly built over a spring of pure water. The owner of the Willow Spring House, demolished when preparations were being made for the mall's building, bottled water from this site. The Nashua Mall, now a strip mall, had opened in 1969 on former farm land. This mall was the first inside mall in the State of New Hampshire. The Royal Ridge Mall is near the Old South Burying Ground and old Brick Schoolhouse.

Nashua Mall

Max Silber worked in the foundry business for many years, but he is best known for his association with the Boy Scouts. In the 1940s he helped found the scouts' Camp Carpenter in Manchester. Silber was Temple Beth Abraham president for sixteen years. He was the first recipient of the YMCA's Man of the Year award. The United Way's distinguished service award is in Max Silber's name.

Reverend Peggy Smith ran the Tolles Street Mission for almost two decades after opening the French Hill storefront mission in the late 1980s. Over the years food, clothes, shelter, transportation, counseling, and more were provided. A Saturday / Sunday school and yearly Christmas Party were offered as well. Smith taught, "If you stand for nothing, you will fall for everything." Reverend David Smith, Smith's son, and his wife continue his mother's work.

Dr. Everett Tuttle, Jr. practiced pediatric medicine for almost forty years. He was a founding member of Nashua Pediatrics on Kinsley Street, a choir member of St. Joseph's Church, and a member of the Granite Statesmen Barbershop Chorus. Dr. Tuttle served on numerous committees' and organizations' boards. Another remembered Nashua doctor was William Thibodeau who made a name for himself in lacrosse before opening his practice in 1932. He was an active member and president of the Rotary Club. As a physician Dr. Thibodeau served on the staffs of the Hillsborough County Medical Society and both local hospitals. He is recalled as a caring man at the time when house calls were the norm. (By 1899 the Hall House on Prospect Street became fully staffed and equipped. In 1915 Memorial Hospital opened its Central, or East, Building; in 1994 the name was changed to Southern New Hampshire Medical Center. St. Joseph Hospital began construction in 1908 with the Sisters of Charity administering and staffing the hospital. The original building was demolished in 1937; the newly-opened facility is now the South Wing).

Former view of Memorial Hospital, Prospect Street

The Providers

Wingate's Pharmacy, Main Street

Gary Wingate is the proprietor and fourth generation pharmacist in the Wingate family tradition. Wingate's Pharmacy, Inc. was established in 1900 and has been supplying health care needs for the greater Nashua community. The pharmacy is a nationally certified compounding center specializing in such areas as women's health, veterinary medicine, pain management, and dermatology, as well as providing nebulizers, home medical supplies, compression stockings, and diabetic shoes.

Nashua native Bradley Whitney, an R.PH. at twenty-five, became the youngest pharmacy owner in New Hampshire at twenty-eight with the country's second smallest apothecary on the corner of Main and Kinsley streets. For nearly forty years he operated three area pharmacies. Whitney is one of the founders of the Nashua Pharmaceutical Association, a lecturer and panelist at conventions, author and copywriter of *The Pharmacist* and an American Legion percussionist.

Whitney Pharmacy, corner of Kinsley and Main streets

Dr. William Thibodeau describes his early years: "I lived two houses from the Yankee Flyer Diner. We stopped on the way out, and if we weren't in a hurry, on the way back from a house call. When I came to town, more than half of my practice was at nighttime. None of the older doctors wanted to go out… My first Christmas I had to go over to Hudson to deliver a baby. Snow was up to my knees. In those days-charge of $25.00 for a delivery – night calls $5.00. About fifty yards from the house I got stuck. Sure enough the baby had been born. All I had to do was put drops in the baby's eyes. When I got ready to go, the father escorted me to the car. Those were the good old days."

FIVE

THE CHALLENGERS

*"The collected pleasures of everyday life
fade quickly away unless there is at the heart
of them the gladness of having done something
that has made someone happier."*

-Anonymous-

The Challengers

Holman Stadium has been the location not only for sporting events but also for countless city celebrations. The Stadium, once a wetland area called Artillery Pond, was a memorial gift from Frank Holman to his parents. In 1939 the field house was dedicated to the youth and the people of Nashua. In the early days crowds would bring folding chairs for some well-attended events.

Nashua artists display their creative talents in many ways. The Nashua Symphony Orchestra was formed in 1923 and re-established in 1960 with area musicians under the direction of Royston Nash who retired after twenty-one seasons. The Symphony has performed concerts not only in the Keefe Auditorium but also at Fourth of July activities in Holman Stadium. The Nashua Artists Association sponsors an annual, summer art exhibit at Greeley Park. Since 1956 Actorsingers, a community theater group, has been producing Broadway musicals. The Nashua Theater Guild was formed in 1961; its first show was in 1962. Art Walk Nashua, in its third season in 2007, began as a partnership between area artists and the city's downtown revitalization organization. City Arts Nashua has assumed responsibility for the Art Walk with open galleries, studios, and participating artists and craftsmen.

Christopher Burney, grandson of Chris and Mary Anne Kyriax of the Yankee Flyer Diner, is a theater producer and also a Columbia University professor. "Having worked with everyone from Albee to Sondheim has been remarkable—but mentors like Mr. Gibson, who taught young magicians, instilled a passion for the arts in me. In Nashua I learned how to take the elements from the world and make something new and wonderful."

Nashua native, author, artist, webmaster, and professional photographer Robin Ann Peters is seen in the Nashua Public Library's Hunt Room gathering information for her 2006 book *Nashua, Then and Now*. Ms. Peters works with technology experts, city executives, city-minded townspeople, and many non-profit organizations throughout the city. Peters is the founder and CEO of the Nashua History Foundation and its website www.nashuahistory.com.

In 1946 Roy Campanella had established himself as a star catcher in segregated baseball. Campanella was both a model citizen and a budding superstar when the Nashua Dodgers, a farm team of the major league Brooklyn Dodgers, made him their catcher that year. It had been sixty years since blacks had played major league baseball, and Brooklyn originally wanted to assign "Campy" to a minor league team in Wisconsin. But the entire league threatened to boycott, so it was up to officials in Portland, Maine to approve the idea of integrating baseball. In Nashua's baseball summer of 1946, Campanella had 13 home runs, 96 RBIs and batted .290 with 64 walks. On base frequently, he also stole 16 bases. By 1947 Campanella was promoted to the Dodgers AAA team in Montreal, one step away from his eventual all-star career in the major leagues.

The Challengers

The Nashua Country Club's history can be traced to a grant in 1659 of a loan repayment of land. A pound for wandering animals was located on the northeast corner of the road now leading into the club. A farmhouse was taken over by the city in 1858 and became the city farm and poorhouse. There, the indigent and prisoners with minor offenses tended to the chores. The building was closed in 1908; the club's present entranceway is a version of the original house's front door; the poorhouse was remodeled into today's clubhouse. The Country Club opened in 1916 with an eighteen-hole golf course. Curling was added in 1928; a liquor license was issued in 1940. Expansions occurred in 1961 with a swimming pool and dining room and in 1976 with tennis courts and a maintenance complex.

Nashua native Ken Gidge studied sculpture and portrait drawing at the Boston Arts Institute. Some of his work is in the same discipline as Jackson Pollack. He is self-taught in computer digital art. Gidge is also an inventor, author, talk radio host, art collector, and creator of the largest abstract painting of its type in conjunction with *The Telegraph*'s 175th Anniversary.

Since Ken Mayo came to Nashua from building nuclear reactors in Richland, Washington, he became active in the community. He has participated in the New Hampshire League of Craftsmen, the Actorsingers, the Nashua Symphony, the Barbershop Quartet (the "Diminished Fifth"), square dancing (a co-founder of the Border City Squares), and other civic activities. He has taught advanced science with the Rivier Institute for Senior Education (RISE) at Rivier College. His wife, the former Jeanne Jewett, was born and raised in Nashua.

Nashua native and inventor Lester Gidge considered invention "the highest form of art there is." At fourteen with no money, he built himself a bicycle from scraps. "I knew I had to be self-reliant. I knew if I wanted a bicycle I would have to make one myself." Gidge held more than fifty patents from huge machines used all over the world to ways of doing everything from picking blueberries, patching together a disposable diaper, and caring for flowers with a self-watering planter (once sold on a televison shopping channel). He was past chairman of the Nashua Planning Board and a founder with Valmore Poulin of NIMCO, a company providing machinery and services first to local industries and then to regional New England. The company is now Ultima Nashua Industrial Corporation. With his wife Eileen, Gidge has established an arboretum fund at Woodlawn Cemetery to purchase unusual trees and shrubs.

John Sias helped organize Big Brothers-Big Sisters. He was United Way's 1997 Volunteer of the Year, 2002 New Hampshire's Big Brother of the Year, and a 2002 torch runner in the Winter Olympics. Sias is the author of seven books; his last, published in 2007, contains questions and answers about prostate cancer. In 2005 he founded the New Hampshire Prostate Cancer Coalition and became its first president.

Greg Landry is a former American football player with the Detroit Lions, Baltimore Colts, and Chicago Bears. Retiring as a player in 1984, he began his coaching career as quarterback coach with the Cleveland Browns, the Bears, and the Lions teams. Landry became a local radio host after retiring from the 1996 season.

The Challengers

Fran Tate, Wilfred Michaud, Mario Vagge, "Buzz" Harvey, and Tony Marandos

Charles "Buzz" Harvey, a Holy Cross graduate and high school English teacher, held in 1941 the position of high school football head coach at Nashua High School. He would remain in the public eye through 1968 as the head coach of a squad that would collect 11 state championships. Harvey's football coaching totals a record of 170 wins, 92 losses, and 16 ties. As the manager of the Nashua High School baseball squad, he coached the team to four state titles. In the late 1960s and early 1970s, he was athletic director of Nashua High School.

La Dame and Child de Notre Renaissance Francaise Statue

Georgi Hippauf is an author, radio host, and conservationist. She wrote, edited, and co-authored three books with former Governor Hugh Gregg. Her book, *The Third Century: A Recognition of Franco-Americans*, raised funds for the bronze sculpture in Le Parc de Notre Renaissance Francaise in the city. Her latest book is entitled *The Story of How They Banished Pickled Frogs' Legs Forever*. Georgi also co-hosted Talkline on local radio.

Amethyst Wyldfyre is a multidimensional artist, an entrepreneur, a metaphysical energy healer, a teacher, a psychic, a medium, and a published author. She is a founder of City Arts Nashua as well as a force in Artwalk Nashua and Firefest. Amethyst's latest works are on display in local galleries, and she regularly performs Crystal Singing Bowl Healing Concerts. Her first published book contains fifteen of her original paintings.

Clell "Butch" Hobson, a former baseball player and manager, accepted the post of third manager in the history of Nashua's Professional Baseball Team, the Pride. This athlete, who played for Paul "Bear" Bryant at Alabama, succeeded in bringing two championships and six playoff berths to the city. Before moving on to another managerial position in the Atlantic League, the original home of the Pride, Hobson lent his skills on the diamond to area local youth baseball as a coach. Four of his teams reached the championship series.

After military service, Alfred Lawrence started a photography business in 1948 in the first of six Nashua locations. "We've always been on Main Street and have seen all the changes," said Lorraine, Fred's wife. The business, first named Nashua Camera Shop, became Cameraland in 1961. In the late 1990s two Main Street storefronts were joined into one store which became the largest independent photography store in New Hampshire. Another relocation occurred when son Brian bought a store located further south on Main Street and moved the store yet again. The store not only sells cameras, binoculars, frames, and photography equipment but also processes film and digital cards. "Because we have a lot of people who come in asking for Nashua pictures and information, we are collecting historical pictures of Nashua to put in a reference album," said the Lawrence photographer. Brian Lawrence, Nashua native and Nashua High School graduate, learned his skill at copying old photographs from his father. Brian is photographic editor of *Nashua New Hampshire: A Pictorial History*. Among many volunteer activities, he is a board member of the Nashua Police Athletic League.

Don Newcombe was just a black teenager from the South when he took the chance to play affiliated baseball in Nashua in 1946. His two seasons in Nashua are legendary, not only in the sport of baseball, but in the area of race relations as well. On the ballfield, Newcombe delighted fans with a 14-4 record and 2.21 ERA in 1946, then with league leading totals of 19 wins and 186 strikeouts in 1947. Newcombe returned to Nashua to see a Holman Stadium entranceway renamed in his honor. He spoke emotionally about being encouraged to walk through the front door of the local Howard Johnson's. (Newcombe's experiences in the Jim Crow South had originally led him to Ho Jo's kitchen door on the backside). Future Mayor Mario Vagge gave him and his teammate Campanella a used two-door Hudson automobile to tool around the Gate City. By 1949 Newcombe joined his original Nashua catcher Roy Campanella in the big leagues, leading to National League Pennants for Brooklyn in 1949, '52, and '53.

Mural, corner of West Hollis and Elm streets

Alex Minasian began playing the piano at age five. Studying jazz became his primary focus. He has played concerts in various Nashua venues, as well as in New York City where he completed work on a Master's Degree in Music Performance at New York University. Minasian is pursuing his goal of working for a record company.

Teenager Samita Mohanasundaram has taught India's impoverished village children, sold Make-A-Wish angels, and donated over 12,000 books to needy places. To help fellow students, she started educational columns in her local newspaper. As a professional dancer, she performs classical Indian dance as well as piano in Nashua area retirement and nursing homes. Samita has received several community service awards including the National Volvo for Life Butterfly Award.

Mr. and Mrs. Jafar Shoja and son, Benoit

Jafar Shoja came to the United States from Iran in 1958 under the International Exchange Program and to Nashua in 1968 as executive director of the Arts and Science Center. Holding a masters degree in fine arts, he has experience not only in gallery direction but also as a teacher, a lecturer, a painter, and a sculptor. Shoja has exhibited his works in Iran and the United States. Son, Benoit Pelletier Shoja, a Nashua native and research and data librarian, collaborated with local Franco-American leaders raising funds for the statue of La Dame de Notre Renaissance Francaise by submitting an essay that appears in *The Third Century: A Recognition of Franco-Americans*. He is a musician who plays such uncommon instruments as the spoons, washboards, and guimbarde. He is described as "an unconditional fan of traditional Quebecois music."

Fairgrounds Festivities
Location now of Fairgrounds Elementary and Middle Schools

From earliest accounts to the 1996 Olympic Torch carried through city streets to the present-day fitness movement, Nashua citizens have maintained interests in all areas of physical activities. 1895 records list a Boat Club on the Nashua River. Polo matches were held at the Fairgrounds Track, now the site of a middle school. Unlike today, school sports were limited to boys, but girls did participate in some recreational activities such as tennis, horseback riding, and bicycling. J.F. McElwain Shoe Company sponsored a baseball team, the Nashua Millionaires, listing Birdie Tebbetts as bat boy. Outdoor ice skating rinks were frequented especially South Common, the land now used as an annex to Elm Street Middle School. Many youth organizations such as PAL (Nashua Police Athletic League) are popular today, as well as various youth sport teams. Nashua also has innumerable gyms, fitness, and health centers.

The Challengers

Poet, artist, writer, and teacher Adelle Leiblein developed a curriculum for the teaching of writing that employs art-making as an integral part of the process. Since 2000 she has taught at the DeCordova Museum, a contemporary thirty-five acre outdoor sculpture park in Massachusetts. Leiblein has written for numerous magazines, maintains a writing/art studio gallery in the city, and is on the board of City Arts, Nashua.

Terry Romano is a retired educator and a board member of the Nashua Historical Society. She is currently a trustee of the Boys & Girls Club Foundation, a board member of the area Home Health and Hospice Care, a board member of the Humane Society of Greater Nashua and is an advisory board member of the Hunt Memorial Building Restoration Committee. She is the current owner of the 1799 Greeley Mansion of twenty-four rooms and ten fireplaces located in Nashua's historic Nashville district. This house shares the same builder, John Lund, as the neighboring Abbot-Spalding House Museum.

Greeley Mansion

Nashua Baseball Team, the Dodgers

Raised in Nashua, George "Birdie" Tebbetts acquired his nickname when an aunt said of his youthful, high-pitched voice, "He chirps like a bird." His major league baseball career of fifty-three years included positions as catcher, manager, and scout with such teams as the Boston Red Sox and Cleveland Indians. Tebbets often said, "If you want to be a good manager, get good players." This life in major league sports was shared with the public-at-large by writing an award-winning New Hampshire sports column. So prominent was his take on sports, especially baseball, his annual mid-winter baseball banquet was one of the country's best attended. Thus, the legacy of Birdie Tebbetts also includes the annual consumption of such culinary firsts as George Scott Chicken Pot Pie, Dick Williams String Beans, and Johnny Bench Apple Pie.

Artist Philip Tsiaras, whose parents emigrated from Greece, is a Nashua native and an Amherst College graduate. Exploring the relationship between writing and visual representation, he states, "Each word is a rich world unto itself." He has worked in various mediums of canvas painting, glass, ceramic, bronze, and photography. Presentations include seventy solo exhibitions worldwide. Philip has been the recipient of many national prizes.

Alex Tsiaras is creator of powerful computer images for books, films, websites, museum exhibits, and medical research. His company, Anatomical Travelogue founded in 1998, produces scientifically faithful 3D pictures and animations. A.T. has illustrated a golfer's swing for NIKE and the simulation of drugs working on a molecular level for drug companies. Alex's book *From Conception To Birth: A Life Unfolds* depicts fetal development through digital art and photography.

Dock at Camp Sargent

In the late 1800s a group of women met to establish a YWCA in Nashua. Their early meetings were held in a storefront on Main Street and then in a building adjacent to the YMCA on Temple Street. When the cornerstone for the Temple Street building was laid in 1912, President Taft attended the ceremonies. The land for Camp Sargent on Naticook Lake in Merrimack, New Hampshire was purchased in 1924 as a camp for boys in honor of Eaton B. Sargent, mayor of Nashua and then YMCA board president. Girls were added in 1961. In 1964 the YWCA-YMCA building on Prospect Street was completed. Various sports and activities are offered.

YMCA (1900–1912)

Salmon Brook

Professional photographer Ralph Wright remembers Nashua. "When I took a quiet walk in my neighborhood and ended up at Hassel Brook on Lund Road just 500 feet away from my home, I could see Salmon Brook where I had fished as a child for rainbow trout. The Acton Railroad tracks had long been torn up—before the railroad there had to be the Native American Indians. Salmon and Hassel Brooks provided early settlers with plenty of fish. There was a trading post at 300 Main Street where Indians traded furs for sugar and flour. It stood where K.F.C. is today. The original building was removed when Simoneau Plaza expanded and Salmon Brook was routed underground through large, cement pipes. The two brooks remain, and the Indian artifacts have survived."

Builder J. Albert Ouellette remembers his family living on sandy Lund Road, the old stage coach route from Boston to Concord. In 1932 the area was wild with a forest of red pine trees and brush. Hundreds of stone chips were found, used by the Indians to clean fish. Salmon Brook was loaded with salmon; pheasants, hawks, and partridges were hunted. The family had a garden, a Clydesdale horse, a barn chicken coop, and an outhouse. Since there was no electricity, the family read by kerosene lamps. Following service in World War II, J. Albert returned home to build his first house. He says, "Nashua was the land of opportunity" and began various housing developments. In the entry of Bishop Guertin High School is a plaque in memory of the Ouellette family for their gift of the land on which the school is built.

Greeley Park

Bequeathed to the city in 1881 by Joseph Thornton Greeley as a potential site for a public park, Greeley Park was originally his farmland. Many people helped provide additional land to extend the area. By 1908 grading and seeding had been done, maple trees and evergreens had been planted, and flower beds had been cultivated. In 1911 the stone and cement Rest House was constructed and a fountain and a shallow pond were added. In 1916 a caretaker was hired from May to October, and a stone monument to the "first white settlers locating near here, north of the Nashua River" was dedicated at a burial knoll in the park.

Author

With no formal art background or connoisseurship, Meri Goyette is motivated by a sincere desire to assist artists in exhibiting their works. Her focus: bringing artists and art to the public's attention by constantly pursuing alternative exhibit spaces. Of Meri it has been said: "As distinctive an artist in her own right for having the insight and keen perception to orchestrate and produce…art shows and performances." (C. Rosenfeld) "She's a living treasure." (Carolyn Choate) "Only you see the world through optimistic eyes." (from her children's poem) Her presentations are "Meri-esque" and "Meri-inspired." Meri, herself, has said, "Second only to natural creativity, an artist needs exposure. My purpose is to give the artist a better chance. I'm unorthodox in my methods. I ask for things other people wouldn't ask for. When you're not asking for yourself, you can ask for anything."

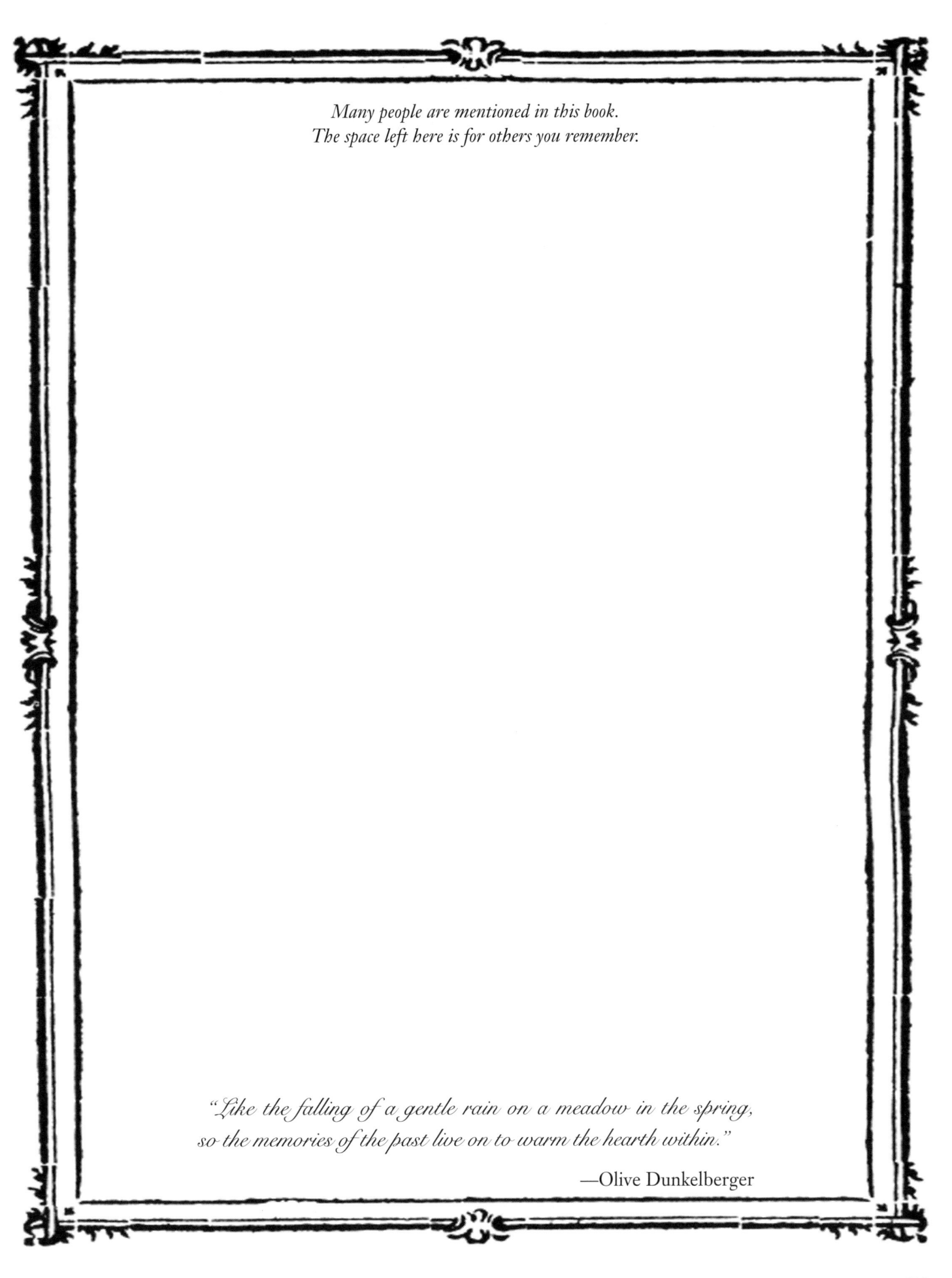

*Many people are mentioned in this book.
The space left here is for others you remember.*

*"Like the falling of a gentle rain on a meadow in the spring,
so the memories of the past live on to warm the hearth within."*

—Olive Dunkelberger

BIBLIOGRAPHY

History of the City of Nashua, NH. Hudson, NH: Telegraph, 1987.

Memory Ideals. Nashville: Ideals, 1965.

Nashua, A Pictorial History. Norfolk: Donning, ©1989.

New Hampshire The Primary State 2001. Gregg Resources, 2001.

The Nashua Century: A Testament to the Leadership, Foresight, and Ingenuity of Greater Nashua. Nashua, NH: Network, 1997.

The Nashua Experience: History in the Making, 1673-1978. Canaan, NH: Phoenix, 1978.

The Telegraph. Hudson, NH: Telegraph, 2007.

INDEX

A

Abbot-Spalding House · 66, 67, 77
Alec's Shoe Store · 6, 7
Amelio, Carl · 32
Amherst Street Elementary School · 70
Aponovich, James · 26
Arnesen, Arnie · 60
Art organizations · 106
Arthur, Rose · 69
Arts and Science Center · 51
Atherton, Ellen Blaylock M.D. · 87
Avard family · 4
Avard Store · 4
Avery Furniture Store · 20
Avery, Charles Holman · 20

B

BAE Systems North America · 18
Bartas family · 26
Benjamin, Asher · 97
Benson's Animal Farm · 28, 56
Berrigan, John "Jack" · 33, 47
Berube, Pastor Paul · 82
Bill, Karen · 85
Bouthilette, Norm · 83
Boys & Girls Club · 40, 83
Buckley, Michael · 5
Burney, Christopher · 107
Burney, Cynthia Kyriax · vii, 78
Burque Jewelers · 6
Burque, Henri · 6, 49, 53
Butler, Suzanne · 34
Buttrick, Wallace M.D. · 84

C

C.H. Avery · 20
Cameraland · 116
Camp Sargent · 124
Campanella, Roy · 108, 117
Capodice, Marty · 55
Caprio, Mary and Vito · 85
Caron, June · 38
Carr, Natalie · 35
Carter, Eliot Avery and John · 8
Carvill, Major Barbara and Carl · 92
Central Fire Station · 51
Chagnon family · 36
Champagne's · 54
Chandler Memorial Library · 31, 37
Chandler, Mabel · 31, 37
Chaput, Richard "Dickie" · 61
Choate, Carolyn · 55, 128
Chuck's Barber Shop · 27
Church of the Good Shepherd · 86
City Hall · 3, 44, 52, 53, 65, 76, 81, 90
City Hospital · 81
Clancy, Frank · 8
Cohen, Jordan · 10
Collins Flowers Inc. · 11
Collins, Peter · 11
Common Crossing Restaurant · 22
Cote, Al · 54
Cote, David D. "Doc" · 92
Crisp, John "Jack" M.D. · 87, 89
Crisp, Norman and Norman Jr. M.D.s · 87
Crosby Bakery · 9
Cross, Robert · 4
Cudhea, Lucille · 33
Cummings, Mike and Gale · 9
Curelop, Sidney M.D. · 84, 91

D

Daniel Webster College · 50
Darrell, Ken and K.C. · 13
Darrell's Music Hall · 13
Davidson, Donald · 53, 55
Davis Funeral Home · 88
Deane, David · 38
DeDousis, George · 47, 92
Diners · 26
Dinkle, Jay Jr. · 55
Dobens, Frederick · 62
Dodgers · 108, 122
Dube, Thomas and Athais · 67
Dutzy, Sherry · vi

E

Eddie's Bedding and Furniture · 20
Elliot, Larry · 12
Elm Street Middle School · 74, 120

F

Fairgrounds · 28, 120
Father Alexopoulos · 55
First Church · ii, 27, 95
Florence Hyde Speare Memorial Museum · 66, 67
Flynn, Margaret · 39
Fokas family · 15

Foodland · 54
Forrence family · 16
Fortin, Charlie · 10
Fortin-Gage Ltd. · 10
Friendship Club · 61

G

Gage, Jody and Jill · 10
Gate City Fence Company · 16
Gaudet, Carolyn · vi
Geer, Penny · 70
Gidge, Ken · 47, 110
Gidge, Lester · 111
Gimber, Betty · vi
Giovinazzo, Dominick · 83
Girls Inc. · 40
Glenday, Charley · 89
Glenday, Timothy · vii, 47
Gottesman, David · 32
Goulder, Mort · 18
Goyette, Charles M.D. · vii, 47, 85, 90, 91
Goyette, J and Judi · 11
Goyette, Meri · vi, ix, 26, 45, 47, 74, 94, 128
Grace Fellowship Church · 82
Great American Downtown · 34
Greeley House · 82
Greeley Mansion · 121
Greeley Park · 106, 127
Gregg, Hugh · 44, 53, 114
Gregg, Judd · 44
Gureckis, Adam Sr. · 41

H

Hall, Norman and Andrew · 88
Hamblett and Kerrigan · 42
Hamblett, Charles and David · 42
Harbor Homes · 41
Harkaway, Aaron and Ada · 43
Harvey, Charles "Buzz" · 113
Hebert, Roger · 96
Hildreth, Isabelle · 37
Hippauf, Georgi · 114
Hobson, Clell "Butch" · 115
Hollis, Morgan · 32
Holman Stadium · 63, 105, 106, 117
Howard Johnson's · 117
Hoyt, Katherine M.D. · 87
Humane Society for Greater Nashua · 85
Hunt Memorial Building · (See Hunt Memorial Library)
Hunt Memorial Library · ii, 11, 45, 65
Hunt, Mary H. and Mary E. · 45

I

International Paper Box Machine Company · 19

J

Jauron, Dick · 9
Jean, Arthur · 54
Jordan's Luggage Shop · 10

K

Keefe, Edmund · 70
Keefe, Mary Doyle · 35
Kelley, Tom · 47
Kennedy, John F. · 12
Kerrigan, Joseph · 42
Klemanski, Majors Donald and Priscilla · 92
Koppenhaver, Neil · 1, 55
Koutsos family · 6
Kyriax, Chris and Mary Anne · 26, 107

L

La Dame and Child de Notre Renaissance Francaise Statue · 114
LaBombarde, Philip · 19
Landry, Greg · 112
LaRose, Dick · 22
Latvis, John and Maida · 93
Lavoie, Robert and Steve · 20
Lawrence family · 116
Le Parc de Notre Renaissance Francaise · 38, 64, 114
Lecius family · 63
Lecius, Edward Jr. · 45, 47
Leiblein, Adelle · 121
Leonard family · 48
Lesieur, Leo · 16
Lesieur, Roland · vii, 16, 28
Levesque, Jeannine T. · 64
Liamos Market · 54
Lillie, Lloyd · 8
Long, Rino · 27
Lozeau, Donnalee · 49, 53
Luna, Robin · 55

M

Mahfuz family · 21
Malkowski, John and Lillian · 55
Malls · 98
Manoukian, Vacchi · 21
Marandos, Tony · 113
Marquis, Don · 55, 74
Marquis, Mary "Shaun" · 74
Martha's Exchange · 15

Matsis, Matthew · 73
Maynard & Lesieur · 16
Maynard, Oswald M.D. · 28, 53
Mayo, Ken · 110
McCarthy, Beth · vii, 55, 67
Mellen, Frank · 67
Memorial Hospital · See Southern New Hampshire Medical Center
Merchants Exchange Building · 15
Mermer, Adam · 6
Michael Timothy's · 5
Milbouer, Stacie · 68
Miller, Herb and Ken · 7
Mills · 19
Minasian, Alex · 118
Mine Falls · 94
Modern Restaurant · 22
Mohanasundaram, Samita · 118
Moheban, Robert M.D. · 47, 90
Mooney, Frank · vii, 55, 67
Mooney, Pauline Noel · 67
Murphy, Carole · 55

N

Nash, Gerald · 17, 25
Nashua Beef Company · 12
Nashua Cemetery · 97
Nashua Country Club · 48, 109
Nashua Emergency Hospital · 81
Nashua High School · 70, 74, 113
Nashua Historical Society · 66, 67
Nashua Police Station · 39
Nashua Public Library · 8, 31, 65
Nashua Trust Bank · 4
Neighborhood markets · 54
Newcombe, Don · 117
Nixon, Richard · 44
Noel, Louis and Melina · 67
Norris, Don · 83

O

Ouellette, J. Albert · 126

P

P E Fletchers · 14
Parades · 76
Pastor family · 14
Peters, Robin Ann · vii, 107
Pignatelli, Debora · 40
Pinet, David and Paul · 20
Pressly, Barbara · 69, 95

R

R.I.S.E. (Rivier Institute for Senior Education) · 69
Reid, Don · 22
Reid, Meri · vii, 22
Rice's Pharmacy · 96
Rivier College · 64, 69, 77, 110
Rockwell, Norman · 35
Romano, Terry · 121
Rootovich, David · 47
Rosenfeld, C. · 128
Rosie the Riveter · 35
Rowlett, Sharron · 64
Rowley, Reverend Donald · 97
Rudman, Warren · 17, 50

S

Sakey, Joseph · vi, ix, 71
Sakey, Shirley · vi
Salmon Brook · 98, 125, 126
Salvation Army · 47, 92
Sanborn, Rachel · 65
Sanders Associates · 18
Sanders, Royden C., Jr. · 18
Sargent, Eaton B. · 53, 124
Savage, Al · 12
Schools in 1800s · 75
Scontsas, George and Ethel · 46
Scontsas, Peter · 23
Scontsas, Philip and Amalia · 23
Sculpture Symposiums/Artists · 77
Second National Bank · 42
Shalhoup, Dean · vii, viii, 72
Shalhoup, Michael · 72
Shaw, Frederick · 27
Shepard, Florence · 60, 65
Shoja family · 119
Sias, John · 112
Silber, Max · 99
Simoneau family · 98
Simoneau Plaza · 98, 125
Smith, Clara · 65
Smith, Reverend Peggy and family · 99
Solomon, Marilyn · 68
Soucy's Market · 54
Southern New Hampshire Medical Center · 81, 87, 100
Spalding family · 66
Spaulding, Forrest B. · 65
Speare, Sceva · 67
Spring, Elizabeth · 65
St. Christopher's School · 89
St. Francis Xavier Church · 21
St. Joseph Hospital · 81, 87, 100
Stabile, John · 24
Stark House (1853) · 93

Stellos, James · 25
Stoncius, Stanley · 73
Streeter, Bernard · 53, 55
Sullivan, Dennis J. · 52, 53
Swart, William and Margaret · 51
Synagogue · 95

T

Tamposi, Samuel A. · 17
Taras Fountain · 77
Teas, Frank Sr. · 47, 62
Teas, G. Frank · 62
Tebbetts, George "Birdie" · 120, 122
Teeboom, Fred · 34, 47
Temple Beth Abraham · 95
The Telegraph · 59, 68, 110
Thibodeau, William M.D. · 100, 102
Thurber, Davis and Patricia · 42
Thurber, Lester F. · 42
Triangle Credit Union · 41
Tsiaras, George and Bessie · 46
Tsiaras, Philip and Alex · 123
Tuttle, Everett Jr. M.D. · 91, 100

U

Unitarian Universalist Church · 97

V

Vagge, Mario · 53, 117
Vale Mill · 19

W

Weidman, John · 77
White House · 10
Whitney Pharmacy · 101
Whitney, Bradley · 56, 101
Williams, Ted · 17
Wingate, Gary · 101
Wingate's Pharmacy · 101
WNDS · 25
Woodlawn Cemetery · 88, 111
Woodruff, Bliss · vi
Wright, Ralph · 125
WSMN · 63
Wyldfyre, Amethyst · 114

Y

Yankee Flyer Diner · 26, 78, 102, 107
YMCA/YWCA · 8, 124